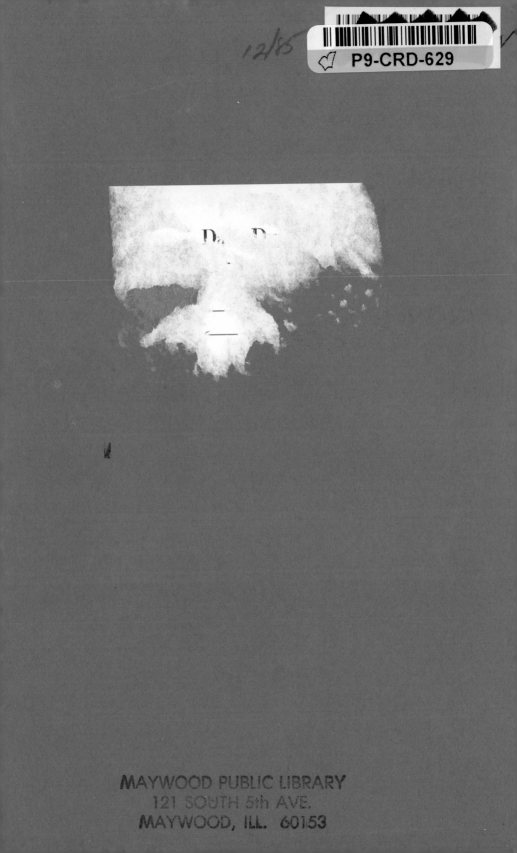

Men and Marriage

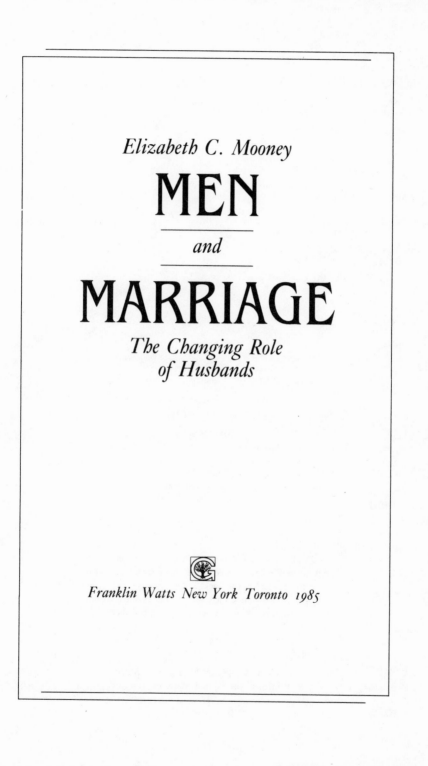

Elizabeth C. Mooney

MEN

and

MARRIAGE

*The Changing Role
of Husbands*

Franklin Watts New York Toronto *1985*

Library of Congress Cataloging in Publication Data

Mooney, Elizabeth Comstock.
Men and marriage.

Includes index.
1. Marriage—United States—Case studies.
2. Husbands—United States—Case studies.
3. Sex role—United States. I. Title.
HQ536.M55 1985   306.8'1'0973   85-13703
ISBN 0-531-09703-X

Contents

Men and Marriage

*This book is dedicated to
my daughter, Joan, and to my son, Ted,
both of whom opened doors for me
to the thinking of their contemporaries*

Preface

In writing this book I talked to a great many people, professionals of all sorts and many undistinguished by graduate degrees, who kindly let me into their lives to share their thinking.

I didn't use questionnaires or scientific surveys, though I drew from some by others. I am not an academic; my interest lies in what makes people behave as they do, in the why's behind their decisions. Rather than write a how-to book, I wanted to hold up a mirror to the lives of people, saying ultimately, this is the way it is with some of us in America today. Many of the people in this book have touched my life in some way, but others I never met until I began to cast my nets to examine the nature of husbands and how marrying affects the lives of us women.

I was extremely fortunate to have a son and daughter who opened doors for me to the baby boom generation and its mores and beliefs. I wanted to know something about the people I interviewed, because I believe that the opinions of people you know nothing of are neither as interesting nor as revealing as those of people you have some kind of line on so that you care what they think. Because of this I have tried to take you into their lives a bit as they speak and therefore into mine. All were given a choice of using their own name or a pseudonym.

Because I am part of the World War II generation and my children grew up in the rebellious sixties, I hope I have at least in part some understanding of changing patterns of man/woman relationships. Though I went to work when war broke out, I number many women among my friends who have never worked. I myself quit my job when I married, so I have a glimpse of both worlds; how it is to be a housewife and how it is to care deeply about your work. And how husbands figure in these disparate settings.

I am very grateful to the people in this book who took the time to speak frankly about things that matter deeply to them.

Chapter

1

Are Husbands Going Out of Style?

My father was a husband, but I didn't think of him that way. That's probably because I scarcely ever saw him sitting at the head of our dining room table with my mother at the foot and my brother and me holding our tongues while they discussed important things. When I was two years old, my mother got tuberculosis and was whisked away to cure in the Adirondacks. I had a dim idea that my father was basically a husband, but in my mind he was more mother/father/ housekeeper and arbitrator of my life.

He didn't marry my mother until he was almost forty, and he told me many times, as I dogged his footsteps from post office to shoe-shine parlor to drugstore, that he was quite a catch. The girls, he assured me, peered admiringly from behind parlor curtains as he drove the black colt harnessed to the phaeton up North George Street, which was the Fifth Avenue of our upstate New York town. He had come home from Yale to go into the family business, and he was in no hurry to get married.

"When I told my father I was going to marry your mother,

he lowered the evening paper, peered over the top of it at me, and muttered, 'Well, you're old enough.' "

The snapshots of him in our family album are very dashing. He looks lean and handsome sitting beside my mother in her big hat and shirtwaist, scowling into the camera in his fishing hat, wearing plus fours and lounging negligently with one foot on the runningboard of his open-backed Studebaker.

I don't remember that my mother ever mentioned how she decided to marry him. There is, of course, this picture of her holding a huge bouquet of stephanotis and lilies, with the train of her white satin wedding dress artfully arranged, turning a Gibson girl profile to the photographer. But she never mentioned the black colt, and on the subject of husbands she was silent.

When my mother got sick, my father was left to keep house and bring us children up with the help of a housekeeper and a nurse. Missing my mother, he dropped in often at the house where he was born—the old house, he called it—where his maiden sister and bachelor brother still lived. Marriage did not especially run in the family. Still, it was in this house that I absorbed the cultural mind-set that for a woman to have a husband was to succeed in life.

Aunt Margery and my father would chat amiably before the fire, forgetting or maybe ignoring me, while my father discussed the problems of running a house and raising children alone. It was here I learned by eavesdropping that he was planning to enroll me in a girls' boarding school a couple of hours away, and here I learned, years later when I was a freshman at Smith, that he feared his selection of girls' schools was ruining my future chances for marriage.

He was very blunt about it, and there was concern in his voice.

"How is she going to drive her ducks to market if she's always locked up with girls?" he asked Aunt Margery, who of course had failed in her own duck driving. Maybe he felt she, of all people, would understand how he might have erred.

Decades later I cringe when I hear him saying this, though at the time I pretended not to hear. The mere fact that I didn't protest then, demand to know why he was speaking of me as if I weren't there, explains something about the era. He was, of course, only a worried father coping as best he could with the realities of the world at the time, and maybe he had a right to worry. The headmistress of the school to which he had entrusted me considered it her duty to guard young women of a vulnerable age, and at school dances, except once a year, we danced with each other. We were diverted by rigorous games of field hockey and basketball from our natural inclination to chase boys. While out in the heartland girls of comparable age were dressing up in miniskirts and shaking pompoms to cheer for the boys' team, my schoolmates and I were personally tossing the baskets in our serge bloomers, working off baser urges of pubescence in healthy strenuous sport.

The message was clear to my father. He was dealing with known facts. Every girl should have a husband. He worried that his decisions meant I was in danger of not finding one.

"He didn't mean you to feel inadequate," says my daughter, who belongs to the sexually free generation. Her judgment is not to be trusted, since she was born six months before he died and knew him only in passing. But she understands you can't judge people out of the attendant setting.

"What kind of indirect messages did I give you about husbands?" I inquire over a companionable cup of tea, our feet resting on Kate, my sweet-tempered black mongrel dog. "Consider what I neglected to say as well as what I said."

She thought this over, dipping a petit buerre in her tea. Ever since she spent two years in England she has had this dreadful habit. Because of her I think of England as a nation of dunkers.

"Go slow," she says finally. "I got waves of messages saying, 'Go slow.' You know, that bit about the power of sexual attraction and how, when it cools, you're just lucky if you find you're married to the right man. It's not strictly true that you don't want me to marry."

"That was not a personal remark," I said. "It was a general observation. Advising a grown daughter is counterproductive."

"I guess I must have been eavesdropping," she says, slurping tea.

And a good thing too. Rousseau said it earlier: Passion and marriage are as unlike as falling in love and love.

I knew the handwriting the moment the blue envelope dropped through the slot. I'd seen it just once in the past forty years, the tails of all the *m*'s pushing down into the line below, the *z*'s and *y*'s with a life of their own below where they live. It was Betsy's handwriting. She lived across from me in Laura Scales dormitory in Smith in 1940 when we were all eighteen.

"Dear Com," wrote Betsy (Com as in Comstock, my name then):

> *Reunion was a blast. Everyone felt relaxed and in good spirits, and none of us tried to impress anyone else with our fading beauty, slightly sagging muscles, or impossible memories. We are all aging and able to laugh about it.*
>
> *There were about 135 classmates at the dinner and, when I asked them as you requested, how many were married by 28, just about every hand went up. . . . I was quite surprised at the response.*
>
> *[Then I asked] how many of our daughters were married by 28. It was impossible to count hands quickly and accurately, so we estimated 25 out of the 135. How about that for a switch?*
>
> *Off to grab a vacuum before the temp gets to 90.*
>
> *x x x Betsy*

There you have it, hot from the presses, the changing styles in marriage. Nationally, the average age for a woman to marry when Betsy and I were graduating from college was twenty-one. In 1982 it was twenty-two, but that doesn't tell the story. In 1983 there were 1.9 million POSSLQ households—people of opposite sex sharing living quarters. POSSLQ households were unthinkable before World War II, and I'm not entirely sure our classmates would have been quick to admit being mothers of POSSLQs even in 1984. Still, from only half a million POSSLQs a bit more than a decade ago, the number of POSSLQs has more than doubled. And that doesn't include POSSLQs of more than two people. Four percent of all couples living together are not married. Says Steve Rawlings of the Census Bureau: "There is no question that in the 28–29 age group, it is more common now to find women who have never married."

"Well, of course," says Kiki, Joan's close high school friend, sitting on my sofa and sipping wine and crossing long, purple-stockinged legs. "I'm a POSSLQ. Andy always introduces me that way. Hardly any of my friends are married."

"Karen is," points out Joan, who is neither fish nor fowl because she lives with four other people of mixed gender.

"Yes, but that's an anomaly," says Kiki. "And she *was* a POSSLQ. With somebody else."

I wouldn't want these long-legged professional women to know how impressed we were back in Laura Scales House in Northampton, Massachusetts, when one of our group came back from spring vacation junior year with a diamond on her third finger left hand. We felt she was now different, crossed over from our schoolgirl world into the real. At bull sessions she was more reticent with her confidences, as befitted her new status. She knew things we did not, and we were respectful. If Smith had had such things, we would have voted her most likely to succeed. Most likely? Gracious, she *had* succeeded.

Kiki's mother is a close friend of mine. In fact, she's a close friend of mine because I hated driving Joan to school every day and advertised for a car pool on the school bulletin board. We're still good friends, though she has divorced her husband and moved west of the Rockies to start a new life. I call her every couple of weeks or so, and the phone rings thousands of miles away out in the great western never-never land, which never seems quite real to me even though I lived in Dallas for seven years, and we talk just as we always did. What kind of a mind-set, I wonder sometimes, did she give her daughter about husbands?

"There's no question that the divorce of your parents influences your own love affairs," says Kiki. "And the less than perfect marriage that precedes it. One of the main jobs of therapists is to keep us free of this overhang. Remember Trudy? I lived with her before Andy and I were POSSLQs. Her parents had such a perfect marriage she had trouble setting up a marriage in this shadow. She hasn't married. Her ideal is too demanding."

The wine goes around again, and Kiki and Joan fall to discussing why Joan's elderly Fiat coughs and shudders at stop lights. They might meet for lunch on Tuesday if Kiki's brochure is wrapped up at the printer's. Meanwhile I am transporting myself back to the Knox School for Girls circa 1935, and in the high-ceilinged dining hall we are consuming hefty slabs of pie before going to evening study hall in our dinner uniforms.

"Name the corners, but don't tell," my friend Bunny is telling me. "Whichever one I tell you to eat first, that's the man you'll marry."

"Well, of course, husbands are less of a necessity now," says Georgia, an old college friend with whom I am lunching in one of Washington's better hamburger restaurants. "No girl has to marry now. She can support herself, has complete sexual freedom, can even, if she wants, have a child without a husband."

She's right, of course. Births among single women jumped 21 percent from 1978 to 1981, and these figures surely include some who became mothers by choice. Famous Dr. Spock, guru of the mothers of the fifties, has been quoted as saying, "A single person may be as good a parent or even a better parent than a married person if the child is especially wanted." Single motherhood obviously could present problems in the dating scene, but the very fact that the possibility exists is another building block in the mountain of options offered women. Before World War II, having what we used to call an affair was not only something you kept as quiet as possible, it was also risky. No high school courses in hygiene or sex were offered us in the forties, and if my mother was typical, you didn't get much help at home. "How can you tell if a baby is a boy or a girl?" I asked my mother. "Don't you know?" she replied and that closed the subject. I picked up the news about menstruation in summer camp.

Hotel clerks in wartime were always suspicious and, in the better hotels, fatherly. Once at the Ritz in Boston a beau of mine escorted me to my room to get, I'm almost sure, a letter from his sister I had forgotten to bring to dinner. By the time I pushed the key in the door the telephone was ringing. "Miss Comstock, do you have a gentleman in your room?" the room clerk's polite voice was asking. "If so, will you please ask him to leave?"

This story makes my daughter smile. The irate father, let alone a room clerk, protecting a young woman's virtue is as outmoded as the scarlet A. You can't order an errant daughter out into the snow when she's a lawyer with a high salary and a condominium with a riverfront view. And of course, it isn't errant behavior anyway if it's the norm. The mantle of social acceptance descends like a blessing on any custom embraced by many.

So then are husbands going out of style?

Dr. Carol Statuto, a psychologist at the National Center for Family Studies at Catholic University and a divorcee for ten years, shakes her head. "It's just that traditional roles are becoming extinct," she says. "Cohabiting is now more acceptable, but largely these partners expect to marry. It's a change in norms."

But Dr. Statuto, let me tell you about my daughter and weddings. She's only been to two, and the first one doesn't count because she was eight and it was her cousin's. It was a very pretty wedding, but it didn't work out. And then no weddings at all for twenty years.

Twenty years. No classmates from high school or college or friends from work. None in her list of acquaintances until Ruth, a high school friend. She even asked me if she should take a present.

No, no, no, I cried, a present isn't a ticket of admission. Think of the problems of transporting gifts proffered at the ceremony to their ultimate destination. Miss Manners, I told her, would have you pilloried.

She didn't know, she says. Okay.

Dr. Statuto, how is it that, if husbands aren't going out of style, the ancient customs of weddings that have united us all for generations are such a mystery to my gently reared daughter Joan? I'll bet she wouldn't recognize Lohengrin if she heard it, and if I told her brides traditionally wear something borrowed and something blue, she'd ask me in what country. The Pocono Mountains resort people claim 1 percent of Americans are getting married at any given hour, but the young urban professional woman probably doesn't weigh in very heavily.

"When our class of 1973 at Cathedral School started high school, we were taught we could have it all," says Karen Kalavritinos Poppadeus, chairman for the class's tenth reunion in Washington, D.C. "It was understood that we could have a career, be a wife and mother, anything we wanted. And we believed it. Somehow it didn't work out quite that way. It was difficult to reconcile it all. Men were intimidated by our expectations. Getting married forced us to give up some of the things we thought were right.

"After the tenth reunion some of us stayed and talked, and you heard that often. Only thirty percent of our class is married now, eleven years out. We kept wondering why there weren't more of us. I'm one of the thirty percent, but I'm divorced now. I think my parents' strong marriage of thirty-five years or whatever made me more impatient with a weak substitute. I don't think men are made of the same stuff they were a generation ago. It's funny how many of us admitted we were looking for a man like our fathers."

Karen is speaking of options. Options not offered Becky Sharp or Jane Austen's Bennett girls, so anxious to catch the eye of Mr. Bingley. Options generally considered until World War II changed all accepted ideas, compromises for young women not naturally endowed with qualities to attract husbands. My own father, whom I still miss in odd moments on most days though he has been gone close to thirty years, had a strong belief that teachers' colleges were for young women destined for spinsterhood. "Normal schools," he would mutter under his breath as we drove by them on small excursions in upstate New York. "Gracious."

It must have cost him some soul searching to send me to Katherine Gibbs school for secretaries after I graduated from Smith. He was trying to provide me with options, but I think it bothered him. "Every girl should know how to earn her own living," he said when he announced his decision. (I, of course, wasn't asked.) Work for women born in comfortable circumstances was a revolutionary idea in his circles.

There I was, twenty-one years old, and still not understanding that it is possible to question my father's decisions. I can't say I felt like Alice Adams going up the stairs to the business school, but I did feel disenchanted with the idea. It didn't work out. It turned out to be a very expensive way to teach me typing. No doors of opportunity swung wide as a result of Gibbs, and when the war broke out I got a job as a newspaper reporter. It took me a month or so to learn how to compose on the typewriter, so deeply had secretarial school ingrained in me that my only control over the typewriter would be to check the spelling of the words my employer dictated.

My mother and her friends, my courtesy aunts, had never, of course, earned money in their lives. They understood and accepted that their influence on the world came through their husbands. The message drifting down to me from being wedged between them in the back seats of their cars on shopping expeditions to Utica or Syracuse was that husbands were rather dear and splendid to have around, not too bright about things that matter—except, of course, money—but easy to set straight and pleasant company. They laughed a good deal about their oddities and spoke of them affectionately. I was shocked when I found some of my mother's old letters to my father reporting that she had seen the suffragettes on Fifth Avenue and thought them "quite amusing."

Not one of her friends would have suggested in my presence that husbands were essential. That would have been in bad taste; it would not have been proper to talk about such things. They pulled the lap robe close over their knees and discussed hats. Still, I knew they were hoping that I would find a good husband. That was what one did.

"Of course, that's how it was," says my friend Ruth, brought up in the suburbs of Boston. We didn't know each other then. She came into my life when we were both married and pushing baby carriages.

Like me, Ruth is a product of strong-minded schools. She was not the belle of the Boston Cotillion where her parents launched her social career. "Don't you want to dance with Ruth?" the cotillion head would inquire ingratiatingly of platoons of small boys a head shorter than she, leading them determinedly toward her chair. "Mother and father were concerned," she says. "I think it worried them that my infrequent romantic encounters never resulted in an engagement ring."

She laughs and dabbles her feet in the country club pool where we are sitting. "I was voted the most responsible in my class and I wanted to be voted best legs."

There we were, Ruth and I and thousands of other young women like us, compressed into our parents' expectations where we didn't always fly. And feeling a bit inadequate because of it. The options that surround our daughters dazzle us.

Here, take my hand and let's visit one alternative to marrying, an 1850 row house in Washington, D.C., on the edge of one of the most famous dope corridors in the world. Such a nice house. See it over there, the one with the bow window and the little iron fence edging the pocket handkerchief garden. Looks like an aging beauty down on her luck, with the paint peeling from the window frames and the front door, with a deadbolt lock, slightly askew. The garden next door is neat as a pin and boasts a lovely rosebush. That belongs to Shorty. He's retired and sits in a chair in the front yard a lot after he pulls weeds. That rosebush is his pride. Those are weeds in the garden of the house where we're going.

I know all of the people in this house. As a matter of fact, one is my daughter. She lives here with Beth and Will and Oliver and, well, the other one is new and I forget his name. Oh yes, John. The inhabitants of this house come and go, though not really as often as you might think. People move away or move on or out of this house.

Nobody in this nice old row house in this block that is sure to be gentrified soon is a husband or has a husband. Everybody is of prime marriage age. But for various reasons they are marking time first, and the Census Bureau calls them "mixed groups." The bureau doesn't know or care why young people form mixed-group living arrangements, but I know some of these sharers, and I can tell you it's because they haven't found the right life partner, they don't want to live with their parents, and they have no appetite for an efficiency and solitary living. That it's cheaper is a bonus.

Such an arrangement would surprise my mother and Ruth's mother and even surprises some of my contemporaries whose children grew up before the sixties. They tend to think that since there are mixed genders involved that old roof covers an R-rated docudrama. In actuality, roommates of this sort do not usually dally sexually. Romantic affairs are kept separate, and "sleepovers" are taken casually if they don't eat too much and upset the budget. Everyone in this particular house kicks in $50 a month for food, which is cooked by duty rotation. The housekeeping chores get done as they get done.

It's a friendly group, and replacing a member of this unofficial family is basic stuff, somewhere between interviewing a fraternity prospect and an encounter session. Nobody smokes in this house; all are vegetarians. Work in fields that benefit humanity is favored. The plants, nearly always in a late stage of near-death from thirst, droop pathetically, the wall paint hangs in strips from beautiful old moldings, the marble fireplaces are boarded up, the cat is not always fastidious about her toilette. But nobody is hung up on perfection in housekeeping, and things rock along in friendly fashion. This is an eighties answer to the impersonality of the world and the difficulties of being sure that love is for real. Friendship and support are what it offers, and you find very little petty irritation.

The youngest here by far is Beth, who at twenty-one, is just out of college. She's busy with the Committee for Creative Non-Violence, and for her group living is a natural progression from coed dormitories. Oliver, the oldest at thirty-one, prefers this to an efficiency and represents the group in its dealings with the landlord. When one of the group gives a party, the others are free to invite their friends too. All know how to reach each group member at work and even their parents in an emergency, and they share everything from the gas bill—in hot dispute, with the thermostat secretly prodded up and down—to emotional crises. Recently, when Joan's place of employment lost its funding, her housemates showed up as free labor to type letters soliciting more money.

Each has his or her own bedroom but all share a single bath, which was clearly enough for the nineteenth-century head of the household but requires a strict schedule for five people going different ways. I keep trying to envision what this undoubtedly autocratic husband and father would think if he could see the crew currently in possession of his handsome old domain. I imagine him with a drooping moustache and cane, waited on by servants who slept in the basement, a gentleman waving good-bye after breakfast to a row of proper children ranged in the bow window to wave him off for the day.

"Group living," says Dr. Margaret Hall, chairman of Georgetown University's sociology department, "is healthy. It sets a pattern for the two sexes to see each other as friends. It's probably based on economic needs, a period before marrying when you're gaining status."

If status accrues from economy, these nice young people have it made. The grapefruit plant I gave Joan after nursing it from a seed to a liability has folded its leaves from the chill of her room. In Will's bedroom there is easily a foot's clearance from the edges of his mattress without bedstead to the walls of the room. And there's nothing like the status of being scheduled first in line for the bathroom in the morning, a prerogative undoubtedly ceded without question to the man of the house in that long-ago 1850 household.

Sometimes Kiki comes to this house, bringing Andy for a party and toting a bottle of very good wine as a gift because she is a POSSLQ benefiting from the blessings of two incomes and no dependents except a large, rambunctious dog. She is usually worried about staying too long lest the dog, who spends the day alone, be unable to hold out. The house where Kiki and Andy live is quite different from this house, so redolent of proper nineteenth-century beginnings, so stalwartly surviving in a changed world. Kiki and Andy's house is newer and has not come down in the world in the same way. It is furnished with things given to Kiki by her mother and with most of Andy's parents' furniture, since they have given up their own house and taken an apartment.

It might be any young married childless couple's home. All of the signs of parental love and approval are there, laundry freshly washed and folded at Kiki's mother's house, dishes on loan, family portraits. But there is no ring on Kiki's finger; there are no wedding presents in the house. The telephone directory lists two names.

About the only thing we're sure about in the POSSLQ relationship, the 1.9 million husbands who are not husbands, is that each stands alone, falling into no pattern. Four percent of all of the men who live with a woman as a couple have made no legal commitment, says the Census Bureau. Turn it around, and neither have 1.9 million women. This eighties alternative to marriage has left a lot of puzzled parents. It is pretty well agreed that you can ask your daughter how much money she's making, possibly her preferred contraception method, but not by the wildest imagination can you blurt out, "Are you and Joe ever going to get married?"

I did know one mother once who did ask, and her daughter replied, "Not unless we want to."

We sit, my daughter and I, in Germaine's, our favorite restaurant of all the eateries in Washington, awaiting Kiki and Andy. Kiki, Joan, Kiki's mother, and I have come here for years to celebrate the holidays, the birthdays, the college acceptances, the business successes that touched our lives, almost since Germaine's first opened. We have been witness here to the virgin birth of a banana to the unfertilized banana plant under the skylight, we have discussed as seriously as the foreign policy of the administration whether chicken Germaine is better than beef Szechuan, and the sate hors d'oeuvres (Asian tidbits) permissible in the light of the news from the bathroom scales. It is here that I first noticed that Kiki's mother had removed her wedding ring, here that I confided to her that my husband was desperately sick. This is a place where we feel at home, and now it is not Kiki's mother but Andy who will make it a quartet, because Kiki's mother has moved West.

Kiki joins us first, wearing a hat and a loose sweater that makes her look like Annie Hall. Andy comes later, sliding into his chair in mock exhaustion, hair slightly awry over a misleadingly innocent-looking face that conceals a razor-sharp mind.

"I'd like a scotch," he tells the waiter, "and one for my wife as well." He leans forward to place a chaste kiss on Kiki, who accepts it as if they had been married a decade. This is obviously a strong and deep relationship. Why then is Andy a POSSLQ and not a husband? It seems so charming and right, their relationship, which sociologists call cohabitation.

"Cohabitation statistics do not lead us to believe trial marriages will deepen into marriage," says Dr. Hall. "In some cases yes, but not often. I'm not talking about morality or legality, but the stress that is more difficult to resolve when the commitment is less. There are conflicts in the traditional notions of husbands. The demographers make it clear young women are delaying marriage."

Maybe so. Sociologists have broader points of reference than most of us and chart trends from these viewpoints, extrapolating beyond the scope of laymen's personal lives. They make graphs while we ordinary mortals have only the windows of immediate experience. But I know of at least two liaisons that grow deeper and stronger every year, which I would not risk a dime betting would develop into actual marriage. Yet they have outlasted many certified marriages. These husbands who are not husbands are deeply committed. There is risk in equating shallow sexual pairings with POSSLQs who, for reasons best known to themselves, are avoiding the altar.

The sexes seem in agreement on the loose arrangements of today. Nobody lays traps to get married anymore. That sort of maneuvering is as outmoded as derbies and bustles, as unthinkable as hope chests. The eighties women seem as ambivalent and anxious to examine the pitfalls and drawbacks of marriage as the men who might be their husbands. They have hidden battle scars from family examples of failure, and with total freedom open to them and psychiatrists to help them work it all out, they appear to be content. Thinking it over is the watchword. A husband is no longer the only ticket to a happy life.

If you listen to the talk, you'll think there's something in the air that wasn't there before—something that breeds ambivalence, makes simple things complex.

There's Laurie, for instance. She's a POSSLQ of two years' standing, toying with marriage. She worried that she didn't know enough to make a decision about the man she was sharing quarters with, that her experience was too limited. She was, she said, first living at home, then with a woman friend from college, then as a POSSLQ. She'd never lived alone. It bothered her, and she sublet an efficiency as an experiment. She made a real effort not to see the POSSLQ during the test. In the end she decided nothing. She went back to her lover with no clear plans for making him her husband.

"I'll know," goes the old song, "when my love comes along, I'll know." The songs of the forties and fifties are full of love that sweeps all before it in a crashing wave. "I took one look at you," wrote George Gershwin. "That's all I meant to do, and then my heart stood still."

"I used to think I'd know," says Louanne diMauro, a 28-year-old lawyer in Chicago. "I'm not so blind now. You're lucky if you figure that out and step back. I thought I was in love twice before, but it wasn't it. It's easy to throw that word 'love' around."

Louanne comes from a second-generation Italian family, and the message in favor of marriage was very positive. Her mother did not go to college and she does not work. Her parents' marriage is happy. The vibes all say marriage is happiness, husbands desirable. But so far the men in Louanne's life haven't rung any bells.

Careers may muddy the waters, complicate choices. Louanne is a lawyer, right at the top of the pay scale, status cloaked. It narrows her choice of husbands because few women marry down, out of their class. Her mother did all the housework, but law is a demanding profession. Back in the house where she was born are a grandmother and a mother who know a husband is what every woman needs. But in Louanne's Chicago apartment these messages get wrapped up in the realities of the eighties, in choices.

"I don't deny it," says Louanne. "I'm like my mother in subtle ways. My mother has her power in her own way, but I'll be different because I'll work."

"Choices today are so much wider than they ever were," says Dr. Hall. "I think two incomes are the norm, and the middle class has the toughest difficulty because, unlike the lower classes, it's not one career and one job or even two jobs. It's two careers. Women are caught with all the conflicts involved."

That husbands have dropped from being the unabashed number-one goal of women in the eighties is documented in a telephone poll taken by the *New York Times* in November 1983. The poll, sponsored by Virginia Slims, found that though 53 percent of women polled in 1971 thought motherhood, implying a husband, was devoutly to be wished, only 26 percent did in 1983. Thirteen years ago women considered work simply useful for getting money, enjoyable to only 9 percent. But work-related pleasure jumped to 26 percent in 1983.

"Ever hear any husband telling his wife he wished he could stay home and take care of the kids?" asks Kiki.

The *New York Times* poll reported that 58 percent of American women would rather go to work than stay home, even if they could afford to. Thirty-one percent more, who don't have jobs, wish they did. We've come a long way, baby, from our mothers' choices. Even 43 percent of waitresses, maids, and factory workers wouldn't stay home, aching feet and all, if they could.

Then there's the pill, which has removed fear of pregnancy from sexual relations. You don't need a ring on your finger to enjoy complete sexual freedom. The worries now are more in whether you should choose the pill over less risky, more old-fashioned means of contraception like the diaphragm. Forties women didn't have any such choice, and we usually learned everything we knew about contraception from the men we fell in love with. I knew better than to ask my mother.

In 1939 Smith College included in its Religion 3 course, among other things, a description of various means of birth control. Other ground-breaking subjects also were included, but they elude me now. I remember only that the course was considered unusually strong-minded and that my father, having heard whispers about it in his club in New York, attended one class when he came to visit. He returned to report to his friends that, not to worry, no one was paying the slightest attention anyway.

The lot of women is improved in other ways. We don't have to conceal brains anymore in order to marry. Beatrice Bishop Berle, in her recent autobiography, said her mother reminded her frequently to take care not to look like a "bluestocking or no man will look at you." One of my own friends tells me her parents were uneasy about her good marks at Barnard. She was already showing unusual spunk, for a girl, and they hoped she would not add to the difficulties of landing a man by being a scholar.

In the let-it-all-hang-out eighties we're emancipated from concealing our brains and our sexual needs, and we're out of the closet about liking to work outside the home. We've rejected our mothers' mind-set, and no law prevents us from adopting or having children without a husband. We can even team up with a stranger to share a two-owner house mortgage. Male companionship is easy to come by on a footing of respect if you keep out of singles bars.

You could argue, if you don't care much what you say, that women can do nicely without husbands.

The laughter that would greet this would not be exclusively male.

Chapter

2

*How and Why
We Marry*

Choices there may be, but as Dr. Penelope Russianoff, a Manhattan psychiatrist with a private counseling practice, who portrayed the psychiatrist in *An Unmarried Woman*, says, "Few are the women who can be really happy without a man." And most of us prefer to marry him. Somewhere around 95 percent of American women ultimately make the trip to the altar. It's just a matter of when. And maybe why.

When I was growing up in Rome, New York, people were inclined to pair off early, with what the town called "a steady" and the country club called "a sweetie." There was an understood "sweetie rule," which meant an unmarried member could take his steady there without paying guest fees, as if she were his wife. This accommodated a lot of people who liked steady companionship but saw no reason to go out on a limb over it. These weren't POSSLQs, just people who had got used to each other. This custom was confined to the older members of the club. Among the younger set the World War II draft rang at least as many wedding bells as Cupid. Among the reasons why people marry, not wanting to go to war has remained steadily high. Married men were exempt, as they were for a time during the Vietnam war.

Some of us single women in the forties hardly ever met a man who wasn't in uniform. The romantic aura that a uniform conveyed was as heady as wine. The sense of no tomorrow, the need to grab every scrap of happiness while we could, as Noël Coward put it, kept the air electric. A uniform in the forties was part masquerade, part carte blanche. What you were in real life was only what you cared to tell, and let the chips fall where they may. A uniform was an introduction—they were fighting our war, weren't they?—and when I was just out of college, the army air corps kindly established one of the four Strategic Air Command bases in the pastureland beyond where we were accustomed to picnic. While the rest of the country was singing along with the popular song of the day, "They're either too young or too old, either too gray or too grassy green," I, like the rest of the single women in Rome, had the pick of Uncle Sam's fighting men nearby and at loose ends. Some of them, of course, had domestic encumbrances they forgot to mention, but as a reporter on the Utica papers I had a revealing master list.

Sometimes, though, I forgot to consult it, and once, after an evening of cheek-to-cheek dancing to the jukebox at the favorite roadside beer joint, the young captain bringing me home murmured huskily into my ear that he'd like to come in. I said I thought not, and anyway my father was asleep upstairs. It developed into a kind of pushing match with one of us on either side of the door, and when he finally decided to give up, he shouted through the crack the final bit of one-upmanship: "I have a wife in Chicago anyway."

Upstairs in his four-poster, wrapped in his Brooks Brothers nightshirt and hoping for the best for me, my father may have twitched slightly, but he had no cause. Deep in the leaky below-grade branch office of the Utica *Press and Observer Dispatch* I had discovered that I could handle my own life. I was drawing down a cool $36 a week, and my one-legged Italian boss, who wore a green eyeshade, needed me. With the key to that basement office in my pocket and my rickety Remington Standard waiting, I was Somebody. What my elders worried about was no longer of great moment. My father's expectations no longer troubled me. I was part of a world where I was valued for my work, and other things took care of themselves. When Joe pounded his desk with his crutch and complained that it was as quiet on the beat as Tuesday afternoon in a whorehouse, looking at me despairingly, I felt close to the center of things. Air corps captains with wives in Chicago were as nothing to me. I could cope. I had joined the ranks of women for whom World War II opened a wider world.

When Dr. Russianoff advises women to become their real selves as a cultural choice, to take charge of their lives, quit playing social games, and find meaning in work, she is talking about me in 1942. Nobody could possibly find more meaning in work than I did at twenty-three, my feet on the lower desk drawer to keep them from the water collected on the floor, dialing the city's undertakers for the obit column. "Any stiffs today, Doc?" I would growl into the phone, knowing myself to be a cog in a respected business. I was deliriously happy.

"You know we would have hated each other if we'd met ten years earlier," said my husband, Booth, for whom I eventually chucked my beat at the police station, the coroner, and the air base to follow him to Texas.

He was right. It was all, as it so frequently is, chance good timing. Ten years before our marriage Booth was exposing the blunders of Texas politicians for a struggling liberal magazine, helping out at the linotype, and sending money home so his older brother could go to college. I, on the other hand, was painting the light bulbs pink in my friend Dorothy's house because we were planning a party to see if it was true that men grew passionate in soft pink light. I knew that men who did not go to Yale, Harvard, or Princeton—pref-

erably Yale—labored in life under a severe handicap, and I
was fond of letting my left hand droop straight to the floor
while dancing, an affectation I thought sophisticated. If any
of the myriad men who made my heart skip had offered me
a ring, we would have had a marriage to make the marriage
counselors shudder. By some great good fortune I didn't meet
Booth until I had got through this period and he was a public
relations officer in the army air corps. We were happily married for nearly thirty years.

"We didn't have any trouble making our decisions, did
we?" says my friend Helen, who grew up in Boston. "I knew
it was ordained that I would get married. I worked for a couple of years and married Henry. That's what we did."

Well, and that's what we do now too, except that we keep
on working. With all the choices spread before us we know
sooner or later we'll get married. We want to have children,
or we're basically nest builders, or we've done the rest and
it's the next step. And above all, we want a husband to whisper that over all women we are the one he loves enough to
overcome the natural reluctance of the unattached man to
surrender freedom.

"We still feel validated as a person when a man says, 'I
love you, be mine, let me make you happy,' " says Dr. Russianoff. "Women are validated by men. Men are validated by
other men in sports and in business and in acknowledgment
of sexual awareness—the dig in the ribs and the nod toward
the sexy blonde."

Financially self-sufficient, feminist to the earlobes, ambivalent about giving up any of the choices we are offered in
the eighties, we still feel the ultimate honor, the only answer
to a deep basic feminine need is to be singled out by a man
as his choice.

So, what's wrong with this? Well, we get anxious and
worried if we don't see it in the cards; we want to find that
one man, be his girl, his wife. Our grandmothers didn't have
any problems with that. They knew they were slated to take

care of their husbands in exchange for financial protection and exclusive sexual relations. Now we can stand alone and get along fine, except that the world gets to looking gray and empty if the man we love doesn't offer us the final seal of marriage. It's not his name we want (increasingly, we don't take it) or his economic support or public notice of the fact that we're married. It's the warm, reassuring feeling that this man, a member of a sex notoriously skittish about legal bonds, has climbed out on a limb to choose us.

When my friend Vera walks into my living room to spend an evening with a group of my friends who don't know her, I introduce her as Vera Simons, the balloonist/painter, and not as Vera LaPlante, wife of the man following her through the door. In suburban circles this custom is not widely observed, and it's fun to see the dawning realization on the faces of the older women. "But they're *married*. Why ever didn't you say so?"

Who knows? Maybe it's the new chic. The women of the eighties prefer to think of it as putting the emphasis where it belongs—on who you are besides a wife. Which is not to say we don't want to be wives.

Every day Dr. Russianoff sees women in her practice, young successful women in responsible jobs, who are despondent over some man's lack of commitment and what it does to their psyche. Few among us have not listened to sad tales of friends who have found at the last moment a man dragging his feet at the threshold of marriage. Lovers who don't want to be husbands are an old story as the root cause of pain and devaluation of our self-worth. Where do we go wrong?

A chorus of experts is in agreement. Redirect your energies and stop giving in to the ancient desire buried in each of us to claim this man forever. Live your own life independent of staking out a husband and watch life fall into place.

"Women have what, for lack of a better word, we call a

cultural love addiction," says Dr. Ann L. Stone, whose field is psychology and who sees a lot of grief in her work as acting director of George Washington Hospital's mental health department in Washington, D.C., grief kicked up by men refusing the sort of commitment in a relationship that women crave. "By nature, we women seem to be more geared to other people, programmed for relationships. Men are far more apt to have problems that are work related," says Dr. Stone.

"We have to unhook from addictions to men," says Dr. Russianoff. "We're so eager, with all our new found equality, to get commitment from men that we begin from the first moment to dress him up in the best light, trying him out in the theater of our mind for the role of co-owner of house and children, starring in the role of husband." We pretend we don't, but we do. Fortunately, we do it secretly, or the man in question wouldn't even linger to finish his drink.

Men, it seems, are more apt to become husbands by accident.

When Joan was little, I employed as baby-sitter the daughter of neighbors across the street, and I think I have even forgiven her for inviting poor trusting Joan to play 52-pickup and scattering across the rug a pack of cards calculated to keep Joan busy while she read. When the baby-sitter herself married, I was at the reception, and I remember hearing how the night Tom proposed himself as husband he went home and woke his family to tell them he was going to get married.

His parents sat up sleepily in bed, smiling approvingly, since they had loved the girl for years.

"But Tom," chided his mother gently, tucking the coverlets around her feet in the cool of the early dawn, "why didn't you tell us you were planning to marry Sara?"

"I didn't know myself," replied the prospective bridegroom thoughtfully, as if he had just discovered it. "I just meant to take her to the movies."

Right here we have a basic parable about the fundamental differences in the sexes. Imagine a woman not having given the matter thought. And when you're through with that, you can imagine Amtrak setting off from New York to Washington with no track.

At every age, in every station of life, we are confronted with basic male reluctance to legitimize a love affair. And sometimes the reasons aren't real reasons but only more of the same basic fear of losing freedom.

Robert Androcki is a thirty-year-old man living happily in a group house with four others of mixed genders, a man still trying on roles and vacillating between career choices. He's a good-looking man with easy charm. I like him and so do a lot of people. In the group he is the one who deals with the house's lines to the outside world, deals with the landlord when things need to be fixed, collects the checks for rent and utilities, and holds up his end of cleaning and cooking chores. An all-around pleasant, amusing fellow but apparently afraid of real love.

I'm invited to dinner at the house. Jug wine, lasagna, and homemade bread served on a butcher-block table under the yawning fixture where a crystal chandelier once hung when a family of substance lived here. The phone rings constantly for one or another of the housemates, but it rings unanswered while Robert tells me about his latest and narrowest escape from the brink of commitment.

He met her, he says, at a party and was immediately attracted to her. He got her phone number and followed up the next day, and in no time at all he discovered the attraction was mutual. They saw each other every possible moment, drifting through the everyday world in overdrive, content just to be with each other.

Then she was sent to the Coast for a week to organize a conference.

We're hanging on his words waiting for the crash.

"When she left town I was miserable," he says. "I knew it was only for a week, but it seemed like forever. The first few days I called her every night.

"And then, little by little, it began to seep in that I was over my head. I was losing control of my peace of mind, and I didn't like the feeling. It was edging into my work. She had too much power over me, and I couldn't face it. I discovered I wasn't ready for that."

When she got back, he took her to the little bistro where they'd often gone before. He poured her wine and asked about the West, but she knew that it was over. It left her, he says, pretty devastated, though it wasn't as if she hadn't seen it coming when the transcontinental telephone calls slacked off. What bothered her, she told him, was that things had gone wrong because they were so right.

We didn't any of us around that table know this faceless woman, but like children deprived of the end of a story we leaned over our coffee cups to demand breathlessly what happened to her.

"Her?" he says, and his handsome face clears. "Oh, she got married in less than a year to a man she'd known all along." He says it in a way that gives us to understand that this is a happy ending.

But the rest of us are not so sure. We think we have just heard another tale of the remarkable agility of some men in locating escape hatches.

Joan is angry, when she hears this story later, at the suggestion that the fault lies with women for expecting what is so hard to come by, so out of character in men. Her eyes flash when she hears the psychologists complain that we must all understand that we are asking the impossible from men in relationships.

"Let *them* change," she says, all eighty-five pounds of her tensed to right this given not properly examined.

Is this possible? Will widespread emphasis on the new male

sensitivity mean that they will be more inclined to offer more than just temporary love without strings? Dr. Hall is hopeful about the new breed of young men now in college who, she says, are far more aware of the value of communication and commitment.

"It's exciting," she says. "Just as the scientists are exploring outer space we're exploring *inner* space. I think that with the women's movement women have become more in touch with the spirit. Men don't have that same transcendence, if you will. There's room for them to grow here, but I think generally there's a whole new comfortableness with being a human being."

Maybe. But there are a lot of us twenty-four and over not looking for college men. And old ideas die hard. The men we know were shaped before the women's movement. They were never encouraged by example or teaching to expose their feelings, fears, and hopes in a way that is second nature to women. It may be the reason why friendships between men are usually based on business or sports connections and remain personally undemanding and antiseptically pure of emotional dependence.

"What do you talk about with the others in the locker room after golf?" I ask my friend Peter. He and his wife live in San Francisco, but we have managed to keep the friendship alive courtesy of AT&T and its competitors.

"Oh, we tell jokes and talk about the Forty-Niners. And the condition of the greens. Man talk," he says.

Peter was a hotshot pilot when Hitler's armies were marching on Paris. He recently had a hip replacement and must ride in a golf cart instead of walking as he used to. The operation was only partially successful, but he rises above the ensuing difficulty without complaint. I'd give sixty-to-one odds not one of his golfing friends, sharing a beer with him in the grill after eighteen holes, has ever turned to him and said, "You never mention your postoperation difficulty. How is it coming? What do the docs say?" And if they did, Peter probably wouldn't like it.

"I don't know that I'd get any satisfaction out of talking about my problems, chewing them over the way Helen does," says Peter. "I like to keep busy with my hands, you know, around the house. I can't read unless I do it when I wake up at night. Oh, there was one book my son gave me—oh, man—all about Hollywood. I read it, and if I can't sleep, I leave the light on. Then I can. I don't know why. Scared of dying, I guess.

"In the locker room we tell stories about the things we did in high school. And later. You know there was this time my old college roommate was on a business trip, and the East Coast contact fixed him up with a deb. . . ."

Clearly, it is somewhere written that among men emotional leaning is bad form. Cover up your problem with the camouflage shooting jacket or the Brooks Brothers suit and tell 'em about the blonde you sat next to on the subway—man, what a chassis and she looked willing. IBM doesn't like to think its men have worries, and neither does your wife. Men have responsibilities. Men are supposed to take care of their women, aren't they, and do their job? Men don't admit weakness.

In a handsome house in a Chicago suburb we are discussing the evidence that men talk less easily to other men than women talk to other women. Evidence is the right word. These men are highly successful corporate lawyers. We women keep silent, sipping the after-dinner coffee as they toss the idea about.

They admit nothing. It is a woman's assessment of unsubstantiated facts. They have friends to whom they speak frankly. Under cross examination the friends emerge as partners. Their world is oriented in business. They are comfortable with partners.

But would you, I persist, lean on them with the burden

of a terminal diagnosis? With the burden of a drug-addicted child? My host shakes his head, cornered. He would lean on his wife. But what if she weren't there? He shakes his head again against such a possibility.

When I call the next day to say thank you for my dinner, I ask my friend is she heard the same messages as I.

"Fred told me to tell you that most of what women tell each other is gossip," she says.

Here's the gossip I hear from my friend Dorothy Caswell when we talk on the long distance phone, weekend rates. Dorothy still lives in RomeNewYork—you have to say it all as one word or people drift off into Italy. There's a Rome in several states in the union so maybe that qualifies it as Everytown.

"When I first married Bill and moved here I felt as if only half of me had moved," Dorothy says. "All the women I met couldn't talk about anything but babies, diapers, and recipes. Then I met you and a couple of others, and we were always able to talk right from the start. We always will be even though we might not meet often or know the same people."

We talk all right. We talk about what she is trying to capture on canvas and I at my typewriter, about how people change as they age, about what makes people happy or unhappy, about suicide and death. We always have been able to talk.

The mail a week later brings a letter from Kiki's mother who has scrawled six pages from a hotel bed in Vail, Colorado, where she is nursing a cold. I have asked her about whether men can talk to their friends as women do, and she is surprised that I ask. Of course, women talk more freely to each other than men do. It has always been so, says her black felt-tip pen firmly.

"We women have always been the nurturers," she writes, and I can see her, propped up in bed on the pillows, sniffling and gazing out of the window at the snowbanks of America's Switzerland. "We have learned to bind small scratches on small knees and small scratches on small spirits as well. It is to a woman that a boy child will admit that the class bully stole his lunch, that there was a party to which no invitation ever came. Because we have received confidences, we can give them. Women can ask for help because they have given it all their lives."

I can see her in my mind's eye reaching for the nose drops and thinking about basic truths. And wondering, of course, if I can find her three yards of narrow velvet ribbon like the enclosed sample.

If Dr. Hall is right, old taboos about strength and weakness long ingrained in men are changing in younger men. In this generation, so reliant on shrinks, the communication that fosters close relationships between friends and, ideally, between husbands and wives, should be on a roll. But there is no tidal wave yet. I've met just one young man who says he's looking for that kind of closeness, and he sees himself as an exception. "Play the field," his contemporaries urge him. "What's in it for you?"

Still and all, in this iconoclastic era we women aren't finding the idea of husbands disposable. Ancient wisdom says the world is strewn and always will be with traps we lay to ensnare a husband, but it's not quite that overt anymore. It's not a search but more like a subtle, unadmitted amorphous belief that somewhere we will stumble over the right man and we will recognize each other. We have large fields to explore and few rules. We can tap our own dance partners, call up men we met at the party last night, look them over at a singles bar, even ask them to marry. If they lack commitment, we learn to cope with that too, maybe aided by the old rule that when a man is ready to marry, he'll marry the next woman he meets. But the wider the field and the fewer the restrictions, the more we seem to flounder. We're past masters at assembling whatever raw material is at hand and dressing it up to suit us.

We may be liberated, but the matter is complex. Eighties

women are long on opportunity and ambivalence and short on clear patterns. Nobody would dare instruct women graduates today as Adlai Stevenson took it upon himself in 1955 to instruct the graduating class of Smith College to go forth into the world and make a difference in it from "the humble housewife status" through influence on man and boy. This was my college only thirty years ago? No one yelled catcalls? Or threw rotten tomatoes?

Women of the forties were quick enough to turn in their wrenches and typewriters when the war was over. We'd held down men's jobs for five years; husbands were what we had in mind, husbands and the baby boom. We'd known all along what we'd do when Johnny came marching home: wedding bells, veterans' mortgages, and baby carriages.

Fifties women knew their minds too, but they were operating in a changed culture. By the 1950s the suburbs and family life were entrenched. Women who married in the fifties by and large had not had mothers who worked, and no war would come along to upset established ideas. The mothers of fifties women, as Andrew Cherlin, the social historian, points out, had been room mothers of their children's kindergartens, full-time mothers chauffeuring to ballet and cub scouts, on tap for their offspring. They had filled no man's shoes during the war, and they raised daughters who saw their future in husbands.

"I talked about jobs for a year in Europe," says Rebecca Loftus, who graduated from Cornell in 1951 and is now the wife of an economics professor at the University of Maryland. "But I was raised traditionally, and my background gave me no toughness. I was timid, too timid to push for a job like the one my older sister held down during the war. The only work I could find to put me through graduate school was secretarial, typing and shorthand.

"I was distressed at my options. I got no example from my mother, who continually deferred to my father. I met Jim in graduate school and got married. I never really worked."

"Oh, I talked a bit about working, going back to school, but I was never serious," says forty-eight-year-old Ruth Adamson, a Philadelphia wife and mother who once drove sports cars the wrong way up one-way streets but now, in her second marriage, is the mother of three, living in a conservative suburb. "In the fifties I was dating, and I had my parents' values in my head. Nice girls don't do that. I wanted to have a fellow respect me. I saw society understood that total freedom would result in a lot of pregnancies. I meant to marry.

"My parents didn't foster independence in me."

True. I know Ruth's parents.

"Isn't she smashing?" her admiring father would whisper in my ear as we sat on their patio and watched Ruth take a horse over the jumps while we drank daiquiris. He never seemed to get used to the idea that he had produced this pretty, headstrong daughter whom he spoiled with gifts and unqualified admiration, while Ruth's mother held her peace.

"I wasn't programmed for independence," says Ruth. "And it took a steady chipping away of what I believed before I was my own woman. I was well into adulthood."

When I think of the marriages of the fifties, I am back in Zion Episcopal Church in Rome as my pretty, dark-haired, eighteen-year-old niece marches up the aisle with daisies tucked in her hair and a bouquet of violets in her hand. It was the first time I ever heard the marriage service altered. When the minister intoned, "Who giveth this woman?" my brother replied, "Her mother and I do," and I was impressed. So was Joan, age eight. It was her first wedding, and Mary was everything she meant to be when she grew up.

Afterward we all toasted Mary's happiness while a man with an accordion played "C'est si bon" and "La vie en rose," and her brother who, like most brothers of my experience have better things to think about than sisters, actually said, "Please take my picture with my sister." It was a rather splendid wedding day, but it fell apart later.

"I married out of rebellion," says Mary, twenty-five years later, from the safe harbor of a second marriage. "I didn't want to spend my life at bridge and golf."

She doesn't say "like my mother and her friends," but the words hang in the air. The decade of "never trust anybody over thirty" was already dawning, and, caught up in the fever of antimaterialism of the sixties, she had picked a Cambridge academic bent on improving the world. With one baby and pregnant with a second, she found herself left by the husband who wanted to right social ills but had tired of his family. When she ultimately remarried, Mary found she was completely happy immersed in a house and five children, letting the world rock along on its own. That's what she was cut out for, but for a while she got mixed up.

In the best of all possible worlds we'd keep in mind that when we swim in the cultural tide we sometimes accept things for which we are ill equipped by nature. What we want today we may not want tomorrow. "I was very young," says Mary, "and it seemed so glamorous, Harvard and Cambridge. . . ." Unconsciously maybe, we listen more than we imagine to buried inclinations that surface when we least expect them to, and we straighten them out late in the game when we have to untangle everything with dependent children, the ultimate commitment, clinging to our hands.

And what do women who marry in the eighties want? Everything, that's all. The whole shmear.

Tick it off like a litany. A career, not just a job for wages but a career that stamps a woman as being somewhere. And a husband, of course, who provides complete emotional support and love born of sensitivity and communication. And no hang-ups if he doesn't make quite as good a salary.

That's important. Twenty-nine-year-old Chris Evert Lloyd, women's number-two-seeded tennis champion, told a reporter in an interview with the *Washington Post* that her husband was the only man she'd ever met who could deal with her success. The odd thing was that she said it in a postseparation interview.

And women marrying today want a man who doesn't feel his masculinity threatened if he changes the baby's diapers. Even this is easier to come by than a husband who doesn't mind sharing cleaning chores; because children basically confirm that a man's a man, but mopping floors have distinctly opposite overtones. And while looking for a husband combining all this, women today need only glance at the divorce rate to see that about half of the marriages of the seventies will, if present rates continue, founder, and that statistic includes marriages enduring in quiet desperation in the Bible Belt and the Dakota badlands. Nobody said it can't be done, but there are realities that intrude.

"I'll tell you about it," says Elaine. "You'll have trouble getting me to stop."

Elaine is thirty-three, a Barnard graduate who has a husband she calls sensitive and supportive. She married him ten years ago and has two children. They live in a two-bedroom apartment in Manhattan, and what she really wants to do is forget the whole shebang.

"All the myths exploded in my face," she says. "The sewers overflowed. It turned out you can't have it all. I was brought up comfortable, but I thought I didn't have those expectations. Now I've discovered that I was enormously resentful that my husband didn't have a full-time job."

It comes out in a rush, these feelings, and you know you're looking at a young woman who has thought it over very carefully and is trying her best to work it out. Elaine hasn't just graduated from college; she's already set up a department in a museum of which she has resigned as head to take care of the children. And she's troubled.

"The women's movement makes you feel less than a woman if you can't manage it all. My perception of myself was that I was very liberated. I'd been living with someone, but possibly because of my European background I was bound by restrictions. I thought that by getting married when it wasn't popular I was taking this big courageous step, but I don't know how conscious the step was.

"My husband was the opposite of my father, and we'd only lived together three weeks when we knew we were going to get married. I never even thought of having children until I was twenty-nine and he was nearly thirty-eight. I quit my job and he quit his. He was a cantor, and he was looking for a career in opera."

Meanwhile Elaine was teaching the Alexander method of dance, which she calls "using the body as it was meant to be used." She teaches on a part-time basis as she watches her husband trying to make his music happen on a business level. Meanwhile the two-bedroom apartment in New York City is $1,500 a month.

"I didn't think of these things before," says Elaine. "Am I being really grown up now that I have two babies I'm responsible for? Children change your life. I think my life would be much less textured without them. And I guess all these things were there before, the way I feel, but the kids change things, make them surface.

"My husband is mostly interested in internal things and in money for what it means in terms of what he'd like. I think the really big issue is we're not used to struggle. My father is a real survivor; he was in a camp. I guess this is my struggle. My mother has a very strong idea women should have financial independence. I never felt my mother was available to me.

"There are so many choices."

Perhaps it's the choices that make marriage in the eighties so much more complex. The mothers of women marrying today had no such choices offered. Even women marrying in the fifties were influenced by the world's view that marrying was what women did, and how else would you support your-

self? I'm thinking of Marian Layton, married now to a man
with whom she has a "comfortable, loving, easy relationship." But she came to this safe harbor from the wreckage of
a traumatic divorce and nine years of living with her present
husband, Ken.

Marian is Tennessee-born and grew up in a well-to-do
conservative family. She had been married the first time at
eighteen, a recklessly passionate marriage, and the pain of the
dissolved marriage was fresh in her mind when she met Ken.
She found she and he were comfortable with the same people
and surroundings, and he simply came to live with her in the
house that was hers from the earlier marriage.

"But both of us felt uncomfortable living out of wed-
lock," says Marian. "We were both conventional, essentially
conforming people. At parties in our Massachusetts town
they'd ask us where we lived and we had different names but
the same address. I won't say it raised eyebrows, but it created a lot of interest."

They got married when her divorce was four years old.
The passion and the pain of the first marriage was behind her.
"It was a more mature love. We are better friends than Harry
and I could ever have been." She works now, having chosen
to be married to Ken and forgo alimony from a wealthy ex-
husband, having chosen a comfortable marriage over a relationship that was at odds with her needs.

"There are plenty of choices in marriage today, but we're
not accepting individual variances from the pattern that is now
fashionable," says Dr. Barbara Cashion, a sociologist on the
staff of Georgetown University in Washington, D.C.

"I think we have to look at people as people and see where
they want to go." The women's movement has made it possible for women to get suitable jobs, but it's as autocratic as
the culture of the forties, when women were told they were
fulfilled only through marriage. You can't stuff everybody into
a mold.

"Some of the most creative women are doing crafts at home and raising children. Pushing papers around in an office in a career may well be not nearly as creative. The women who raise the next generation of children should have real rewards, pensions even. The women's movement must move on and offer a real choice that allows individuality. I think women have been sold down the river."

Maybe what we have to think when we marry—as we usually do—is that it's a growing together, as Dr. Cashion calls it, and that, all things being equal, there's plenty of room within marriage to be true to who you are.

Chapter

3

Love Never
Comes Out Even

"Once I called him for no reason at all except to tell him I really cared about him. He said, 'That's nice.'"

That's Alison Prentice speaking. She's sitting on my sofa, feet tucked under her, wrapped in a blanket because the death of a love affair makes people cold, like a fire gone out. Alison is in love with a man who got over loving her. Alison is a lawyer, on her way up, her future on a roll. She should be walking on roses, but actually her big dark eyes at this moment are brimming with tears. David is what she wants, and he couldn't even summon up the grace to tell her it was over. She thought he was abroad on a business trip until she spotted him across the room at a party. With another woman.

Nobody in this room likes to hear this. Figuratively, we women are circling our wagons. There are plenty of other men for a woman like you, we tell her. Forget this clod, this David. There were others before him, and there will be others after. But she doesn't want others. David is what she had in mind.

She's thinking now, she says, of marrying the safe, unexciting man in her life, the one who has been there all along, in the wings, hoping to pick up the pieces. Maybe the way to live is to play it safe, forget the *coup de foudre*. How long does that last anyway? Long black eyelashes frame eyes with dark circles under them. David really mattered.

Would this be a mistake, do we think? Should she skip love, so unreliable and painful? We don't know, but we think we do. We think we wouldn't, she shouldn't. We think she ought to think long and hard about getting married just to prove something to herself, or just to be married. But we don't tell Alison that. We offer her a glass of wine and a hug.

At any given moment, somewhere, some love affair is falling apart, turning to ashes. Some man is rising up on his elbow to look down earnestly on some girl and murmur that it isn't *really* working, is it? Leaning over a drink in some bar and telling the girl across the postage-stamp table that she deserves someone better, more worthy of her. And sometimes, of course, the roles are reversed and some woman is squinching off an engagement ring to lay it apologetically in front of its donor, looking embarrassed and apologetic but stumbling on nevertheless with the explanation about how she never meant to have it work out this way. But not so often, because women are better at endowing the men they love with the characteristics they find desirable than they are at recognizing the warning signposts in a love affair. We find it hard to take a good hard look at the truth when we've made up our mind.

Reaching for the man who doesn't reciprocate is one of the best things we women do. Scarlett O'Hara set us a fine example, yearning after a highly unsuitable man, hurling an ashtray at the wall in her fury at losing him. But we don't need any examples to perfect the art. We have inborn talent. Scratch any woman's love life and you'll find at least one rejection, and if you don't, she's lying. We're perverse in our choices. Just try to marry Ashley Wilkes off in your mind to Scarlett, and you'll see how we women get off the track.

Why do we do it? Why do otherwise intelligent, reasonable women lose their heads over a man who is not the right one? Why, with the world presumably full of decent, suitable men, do we insist on loving the wrong one, the one who has other plans? And suffering rejection, or worse, later regret.

Because reason isn't involved, of course. Love is a trick of the fates, stemming from nothing more logical than a crooked grin or a gesture. It's a game of chance with the "Tilt" sign flashing, and when we only mean to wade, we drown. The psychologists can't advise us how to pick a man. It's a matter of chemistry, wrapped in gift paper. "We don't find out what we've got for years afterward, or maybe when there's a crisis," says a woman I know who is finding out.

Love never comes out even. The time or the place of the characters aren't in the right moon. He loves her and she loves that man over there and he loves somebody else. Pain. Anger. Rejection. Evasion. And depression. What's to do about it? Dr. Phyllis Grodsky, a social psychologist at the New School for Social Research, thinks that if you can't lick 'em, join 'em. She suggests we women should try to be more like men.

"In the fast pace of the me generation a relationship can end on a dime," says Dr. Grodsky. "We should enjoy the time we have with a man," she says, "and keep in mind the possibility, even probability, that some relationships won't last. Men," she says, "have less trouble with this attitude than women."

"I'm sorry, Gloria, I want out . . . out OUT," says the man on the bar stool, running his finger inside the collar of his shirt. "That early giddy phase of our relationship is past and I wasn't meant for the long-term stuff. I was born to run, baby, RUN."

Gloria is saying nothing, looking slightly quizzical.

"My god, Gloria, I'm *suffocating.* Do you realize how long we've known each other?"

"45 minutes."

"GASP. ACK! AIR!"

That's Berke Breathed speaking through his characters in Bloom County, the comic strip picking up an audience originally hooked on Doonesbury. You can find out a lot about life reading the comic strips.

Almost all of the messages small boys receive when they are growing up involve learning that maturity means breaking away, cutting loose, standing on your own, independence. But we women learn from the first how to make connections with people, learning independence and how to take care of ourselves but knowing in our bones that what's important is having someone you can count on in your life. We learned it, by positive or negative example, from our mothers, and it's buried deep in us, no matter how many rungs of the career ladder we climb. According to the women's movement, we can have anything we want, but we want people. It's a double message.

Alison is sitting up straighter and sipping a second glass of wine.

"I think men are very confused about their role today. They feel under pressure."

We are sitting—Andy (a neighbor), Bill Fripp (a visitor), and I—around the table in my kitchen talking about life, as Andy, who loves to work with his hands and reminds me of an idling motor when there's nothing in them, tries to pry open the jar of marmalade I bought yesterday.

"Marmalade jars are always hard," says Bill with the air of a man who has observed one of life's great truths. Bill, handsome in tweeds, an elderly yellow sweater, sneakers, and surely the longest graying sideburns in the world, is talking about the way his plans for a second marriage have run off the track.

"Why do you want to get married again?" I ask him as we all watch a squirrel solving the problem yet again of getting past a new barrier to the sunflower seeds meant for the birds.

Bill laughs, a charming laugh that says, "Don't take me seriously." He says he wants a nurse for his old age. We laugh with him to show we know he's joking. He won't get old anyway; we know that. He's fifty-five and always will be.

"Seriously," he says over the rim of his coffee cup, "I want to get married. I've been living with this woman for seven years. I don't want that anymore—too many escape hatches, too easy. I got her a ring and everything. We had the blood tests. She got cold feet two days before we were going to do it. I was devastated."

Andy has the top off the marmalade and has moved to my bread drawer, tightening the screws. He's not really listening, but perhaps he's heard it all before.

"What was the matter with the first marriage?" I ask Bill, watching the squirrel draped in a sinuous coil around the feeder while a ring of sparrows make do with the hulls he drops to the ground below.

He hasn't any doubt.

"Too young," he says at once. "There should be a law that no one under thirty can get married. You know, every single person from my first wedding is divorced. We got out of Harvard in the early fifties. My generation finds the women's movement intimidating—these women who want careers too."

"I am very tired of men under pressure, confused by their role," says Joan, looking at Alison. She says it with such feeling, emphasizing every word, that Katie, on the hearth rug, wakes up and stares at her.

"Men continue to want—to *need*—to be married," said Peter Filene of the University of North Carolina at Chapel Hill in a paper he presented before a conference on the conventions of gender, sponsored jointly by Smith College and the Smithsonian Institution. "The persistently high rate of marriage and remarriage testify to that." But the culture has left them puzzled about what's expected of them. Tradition, a century ago, taught "manly character" which, as Filene points out, has dissolved into self-fulfillment. "Ambiguity doubled. And it tripled when the roles of women began altering in drastic ways. As the domestic angel entered college and career, and the deferential lady demanded equal rights in politics and law and bed, the traditional gender arrangement fell apart. . . . Men had depended on women's dependency."

Bill, former journalist, currently owner of a ranch in Arizona and planning to write a novel, is now hoisting a gin and tonic, still considering his love life.

"There's another man in her life now," he says, "but she won't marry him. She needs to be comfortable and he can't take her to the Caribbean the way I can."

"I think it's a tough time for women," says Eddie Prieter. "But, listen, men and women are in this together."

Eddie is a friend of my son's, a Denver anthropologist whom I hadn't seen for years till I happen to run into him in a delicatessen on a trip back East.

He's a big, good-looking man, the kind the artist, with a few strokes, suggests as looking admiringly at women in ads for Bloomingdale's more expensive gowns. He looks to me like the kind of a man any woman would be pleased to find seated next to her at a dinner party. He was carrying the Sunday paper and wearing a pair of dark glasses, which he ripped off so I could recognize him.

All the pleasant places where you used to be able to buy a cup of coffee and talk have been torn out of drugstores and sandwich shops. Nowadays you have to settle life's problems standing on a street corner. And so we stood at a light on Massachusetts Avenue and tried to catch up on fifteen years. Denver was pleasant, he said, but his personal life was not going well. A love affair had just crumbled around his ears.

I'm always favorably impressed when people tell you things that matter to them them instead of trading pleasantries, and I made sympathetic noises.

He eyed the stream of traffic for a moment and then gave me a wry smile.

"It's not like having your puppy run over," he said. "Separation is a kind of death."

Standing there on the corner, traffic whizzing by, he told me about it. What struck me when I thought about it later was that all through the story not one word of criticism of this woman, ten years his junior, departed now from his life, passed his lips.

She was a waitress in a bar, he told me, but I mustn't let that fool me because actually there was much money in her background. He didn't explain why she was working in a bar. He just took me from the moment when, whatever the conjunction of planets that brought them together, they met. "I was in high gear," he said. "You're only in high gear for a small part of your life. Going into that bar was a mistake."

Three months later they set up housekeeping in Eddie's house in an attractive suburb.

"I knew it was going to be all right," says Eddie. "I'd stop trawling, clean up my act, get some structure in my life. Enough is enough. We were doing yard work together. I got to think I could break the spell of the trouble in her background—you know, make it all right again."

After a year they decided to get married. Then things got out of sync. She moved back East, and the message was clear. It was all over.

"What went wrong?" I ask him as a truck roars by. What was the catalyst that broke them apart?

He doesn't answer directly.

"I think living together is a mistake," he says and possibly he meant it to be an answer. "I know it's what we do, but it's wrong for the woman. You know there's always going to be that lifeboat. I wouldn't do it again."

But it's more usual to find things drifting wrong when marriage isn't the choice. "Different values?" I hazard.

"That's part of it," he says, shifting his paper to the other hand. "But when you decide to get married a lot of people get into the act, and you get to wondering who's in love and who's already married."

That somehow didn't seem reason enough, but further than that he would not go. On the underlying mistakes he was articulate. The blame was his, he implies.

"I think I was too much of a chameleon. If she wanted this or that, I wanted to give it to her. I would literally have died for her. It was like one of those old Dorothy Lamour movies where they're in the tropical storm holding on by their fingernails."

You can see it still hurts, so I stop prodding and ask what he'd learned, because that's the gift that comes after the fire.

"I'm more comfortable with myself now," he told me. "After a while you learn who you are. I guess you have to grow up sometime, but I grew up all at once. I'm strong now. But maybe I don't want to be strong.

"I came out of it valuing my family more. I have this great desire to give back. I've been in a period of dependency, and I finally woke up to the fact that I was just a diversion. It all makes you feel the way you do when you're on the way to Tiffany and you have to turn your head aside to avoid looking at someone who has thrown up on the street. I see now that we're all kind of standing in a desert alone, but sometimes you can turn your head and find you're not alone after all. But that's chance and you can't look for it.

"It's a tough time for women. There are so many directions for them to go, morally and spiritually. Sometimes I think they're a little too tough, maybe like Anna Christie—you know, pour me a drink. You don't have to wear a suit to succeed."

I wondered if they'd explored arguing it out.

"Sure. And it came down to who trusted who."

I asked him if he'd be in town long enough to stop by the house and have a drink before he went back West, and he grinned.

"I don't drink anymore. I won't be cutting a figure at a disco anymore. You can do that only so long. Right now I want to give something back."

Obviously, love and husbands, reluctant and eager, are complex matters. Nothing is simple. Bill, fifty-five, wants to get married; David, thirty-two, feels the need to escape; Eddie, also thirty-two, has been devastated by the failure of a relationship. It could be that we women expect of the wrong man, at the wrong time, something he is incapable of giving. Or not ready to give. Maybe in some odd way they're saving us from ourselves, knowing they're wrong for us at the moment. Maybe heartache is measured out unfairly but usefully. We're all stumbling toward the same hope for happiness, men and women both, but at different times of our life we're looking for different things.

"Women should learn to see themselves in terms of a whole life cycle," says Dr. Grodsky, "and remember that there are no guarantees."

But Dr. Grodsky, this is not a thing we do well. Once we women dive into a relationship, we pretty much like to think we're more than ships passing in the night. The best we can do is maybe be a little more careful before we choose. But who's careful choosing? Ask Eddie Prieter. Love is something that happens to you. And there you are, stuck with the wreckage.

"Are things looking better?" I inquire of Alison when we talk next. She says she's convalescent. There's a void in her life where David used to be, and that gives her a lot of time to think about David. Victims of broken love affairs may get stronger, but they have need of a new focus.

"What do you mean?" she inquires without much enthusiasm.

I mean new connections. She needs, I think, a new focus. To move on. Learn, as Edna St. Vincent Millay once suggested, the Latin name of every bird ("not only in America, but wherever they sing"), become a Civil War buff, enlist in a cause full of people who never heard of David, study Russian. The heart does not obey commands, but the mind can shout it down. Rejection and disillusionment sometimes are the last twist in the yellow brick road to a new life.

It's even possible to take a wry pleasure in discovering things are going wrong before you have decided to marry. Joy Ray, a librarian in Prince George's County, Maryland, says she hopes her daughter won't repeat her mistakes and marry in haste. "I'm so glad," says Joy, "that now it's perfectly acceptable to live with men instead of marrying right away. You can extricate yourself so much easier if there are no children."

But of course not everybody agrees. Eddie Prieter thinks living together before marriage offers too many escape hatches. The daughter of a friend of mine tells me that she couldn't possibly wish to erase her first bad marriage because it produced two sons who are central to her life. It's a game of chance, and the rules keep changing. The divorce courts are crowded, and who's to say you don't learn through mistakes?

Still, bystanders, like parents and friends, keep wanting to get into it. A generation ago marriage was forever, and parents were the ones who did the worrying about their children's choices. Especially daughters. That his daughter should marry the wrong man was every father's closet nightmare, a man who would make her miserable when she comes to her senses and probably waste her inheritance to boot.

"What do you see in this man?" I can hear my father crying in despair as he struggles out of his buckle galoshes in the vestibule of our house. I have just told him that I am about to marry that army captain, the one who came to the Christmas party, remember? The one with blond hair?

What do I see in him? Why, I see an impossible world without him. I see my future, my life. But I am silent, having no way of saying this to my father who is moving to the sideboard to pour himself a drink.

"I thought he was married," he says, peering at me over the rim of the whisky glass.

"He's got his divorce."

I can see my father still, climbing the stairs heavily, suddenly aged under the burden of the news. He's gone ten minutes, and when he comes down, he shrugs into his overcoat.

"Well, that's that," he says. "Let's go for a ride. You drive."

There's no way to describe the high drama of that watershed moment. Never in my life had I taken the wheel in his presence, his car. He was giving up, relinquishing control of my life, and both of us knew it. He didn't consider I was choosing Mr. Right, but he also knew he had done what he could for my happiness and that advice to a grown daughter in love is useless.

"Do you think," he said as we rounded the curve of the lake near the country club, "that this man can be marrying you for your money?"

I was indignant, but I understood. I knew he was asking it out of fear, out of concern for me, but I was still indignant. He said nothing more on the subject, but he quietly tied up my small inheritance with every legal impediment the law could devise. My father wasn't alone. Two close friends of mine have similar trusts from their grandfathers, money that reverts to the bloodline should they die before their husbands.

The irony is that eleven years later, when my father lay on a stretcher in the hall waiting to take his last trip to the hospital, he called for the unsuitable man I had married. He had turned out to be Mr. Right after all, but how could he tell when I first gave him the news on that bleak snowy day years before?

I was lucky, but all around us are people not so lucky. Dr. Polly Bart, for instance. She made a mistake in her first marriage, and not until she turned forty did she make up her mind that picking the right man is a matter deserving at least as much thought as your career.

So Dr. Bart, Radcliffe graduate with a Ph.D. in city planning from Berkeley, advertised in the personals of a local magazine. She said she was not interested in a sexual playmate but a husband.

She had been dating a great many men, but they weren't husband material. She had been wasting time, she decided, on the wrong men. Though for ten years she had been content to be single, now she wanted to marry, wanted a different kind of life.

"I wasn't doing any of those things the psychologists claim are wrong," says Polly Bart. "I wasn't too picky, too quick to rule out people with the wrong background or not as physically attractive as we might hope. I wasn't too rigid. I was wasting time because it's hard for me to say no to people.

"Now when I say I'm looking for a man to marry, perhaps have another child by [she has a thirteen-year-old daughter], you'd be surprised how many men say they're glad to meet a woman who knows her own mind. I'm more selective now, more demanding. I'm not looking for a man who wants a fling. I've had that."

Dr. Bart feels the kind of man she's looking for is out there, and she's dating a couple of the right sort now. She thinks that most women are not frank enough about their intentions.

I murmur that some psychologists say we women are too quick to cast men in the role of husbands, and she says quickly that the man answering her personal ad shouldn't feel crowded.

"He's free to look for what he wants, but not from me. We should understand each other."

Personals have been rising stars lately in the quest for the right mate. Western rural magazines have long run ads like "Widower needs wife to help run ranch," and women are quick to advertise themselves as strong and willing to share chores that come with a package labeled marriage. The *Village Voice* is said to be the first to publish the personals of the young urban professionals searching for fulfillment through sex and meaningful relationships, but these ads are big in most cities now. Singles bars these days seem to be taking on more of a reputation as meat markets. "Too much up front," says one young man I talked to who met his wife at a Fourth of July celebration on the mall in Washington, D.C. He found her in a crowd of 250,000? She was carrying a backgammon board, he explains, as if that clears things up.

Personals are one way to sort through a crowd for the right one. Computerized dating services are another. Joy Ray tried the Single Booklovers Club, thinking it would bring together people with a common interest. "It didn't work. People would write in and say they loved Dostoevski and fine wines, but it didn't turn out to be true. And I'm not good at small talk."

The under-thirty-five crowd still seems to love to hit the singles scene on Saturday night, where the crush itself is the introduction. On a radio program I once heard an anthropologist discussing a visit he made to the Georgetown section of Washington, D.C. on prime-time Saturday night. He was fascinated. And professionally appalled. Seated in his car he had watched the pursuit, the byplay, the mating dance of the young urban professional, with an anthropologist's eye. He didn't believe in it.

"Those young women were looking for impossible men," he was saying as I caught his message between trips to the library and the supermarket. "And they're looking in a field of men who have already, judging by their age, had one disastrous marriage and are gun shy. And the second time around those men will be looking for younger women."

Mr. Right they apparently are not.

Is it easier to find love and marriage in, let's say, Seneca, North Carolina, Fort Collins, Colorado, or Oneonta, New York? Are chances less for shattered love affairs and marriages in small towns?

"We make our best choices when we have maximum knowledge of a mate," says Dr. Thomas Bowman, a Long Island University professor who has studied mating and marriage and with two clinical psychologists has written a book on the subject. "But unfortunately, Americans are more apt to consider chemistry. Relationships prosper best when both are equal, not just in the money each brings to the relationship but in qualities that take longer to discover than sexual attraction."

This points to more stable relationships in small towns where couples know each other's families and have seen their mates in all kinds of circumstances. But Joan, who spent a year in Seneca, North Carolina, remarks that you pretty nearly have to get married in places like that, so the advantages of long acquaintanceship are not overwhelming. Like them or not, you'd better marry one of them.

"The divorce rates are way down in small towns, but this may be due to social sanctions," Dr. Bowman continues. "But wherever, women have traditionally been at a disadvantage since they have (until recently) brought fewer assets and been forced to trade on appearances."

In a nineteenth-century brownstone apartment on Connecticut Avenue in Washington, D.C., two women lawyers, both twenty-seven and single, talk about this, complaining that parity in assets is hard to find and that for them the field is remarkably limited.

"I have great difficulty getting my dates to accept me for what I am," says Katherine Harrison, a legal contract specialist and Vassar graduate. "I'm not a secretary or a file clerk. I've got a brain, and I don't want to pretend I don't when I'm with men."

"I think," says her roommate, "that men feel more comfortable with fluff. They're in the driver's seat then."

Here we are again with sexual identity turned confusing and parity between the sexes in question. Do these young women want to shed their professional identity in order to attract men who may disapprove of what they really are? Do we women need approval and admiration enough to conceal attributes some men might find threatening to their masculinity?

Sometimes, I guess. I can hear my own daughter saying to me not long ago, "He wouldn't like you if he really knew you." Touché. We're not talking here about denying your principles but soft-pedaling what doesn't fit the picture, and I have been guilty. I don't think I'm alone.

Should those young women lawyers out on a date reach for their share of the check or their compact when the bill arrives? Would they be comfortable choosing nonprofessional men, possibly even out of their class?

Traditionally, men have had no difficulty crossing over class boundaries. It's practically un-American to mention class today, but the movies of the thirties were full of girl-marries-boss tales, and that was when women worked because they had to, not for self-identity or to enjoy a higher standard of living. Power and position were frankly accepted as desirable in a husband, known as "a good catch." Nobody was surprised when a man married a chorus girl or even a five-and-dime clerk. "I found a million dollar baby in a five and ten cent store," went a hit song of the time. Men did that. It was understood. A brain in a woman was not considered an asset. Seventy-five years ago it was mostly strong-minded, not very pretty daughters who were sent to college.

But myriad were the daughters of well-to-do parents who were bundled off for a season in Europe when it looked as if they had fallen for an unsuitable man. And for what are debuts arranged but to ensure that a daughter of marriageable age will choose the right husband from her own background? My college friend Emily clearly remembers that she was sent East to school to, in her mother's phrase, "catch a man." Implicit is the qualification, "a proper man." Sure enough, she married a boy from the neighboring college and was supremely happy.

My aunt Margery, born in the Victorian age, never married, but all of her life she toyed with men who were not considered her social equal in our town. My grandfather, observing this tendency early, hastened to tie up her inheritance as did other fathers of the era, but to the last Aunt Margery occasionally took weekend jaunts with her chauffeur as her traveling companion. Evening after evening my father, my bachelor uncle, and his lifelong sweetheart, Sarah, would gather in the high-ceilinged rooms of my grandfather's house, which had been left to Aunt Margery only for her lifetime, and exchange meaningful looks as the maid appeared to announce a phone call for Miss Margery. (My aunt was pressing sixty at the time, but you never grow up in small towns.) "Heaven send it's the boyfriend," Sarah would say, rolling her eyes, while my father recrossed his legs irritably and muttered, "Hasn't he read the will?" Everyone knew that men may step outside their circle, but women must marry up or sideways.

Now we know no such thing, but something in the female nature keeps prodding us in that direction. Maybe it's a mind-set from our mothers, from the days when men were head of the house, breadwinner, and final authority, and women took their positions in the world from their husbands. The world no longer cares. But what's a woman doctor going to find in a male nurse—unless, of course, an overpowering physical attraction or a man she can dominate. No parity here. Katherine Harrison and her friend are mulling over real problems in finding the right love.

Nothing is simple, and love affairs can go sour not only from lack of commitment and crossed stars but because, as Dr. Bowman points out, both partners don't bring equal assets to the coupling. They're wrong for each other, and besides it's the wrong time and the wrong place, as Cole Porter wrote. You really can't dissect love.

"Younger women are more apt to be attracted to the wrong man," says Anthony Rotundo, a professor of family history at Phillips Andover Academy in Andover, Massachusetts. He feels it's a matter of the culture's accent on romance, a preference, in the words of his wife who is a vintage-movie fan, for Clark Gable over Spencer Tracy.

But Mr. Rotundo, Spencer Tracy was unfaithful to his wife for years. And really, we're not talking here of roués and flamboyant movie idols but only of men who for some reason or another are wrong at a particular time for the women who fall in love with them. Or of women wrong for men. Think of Somerset Maugham's Philip, yearning after Mildred, bringing him coffee in the cafe. "It is awful, love, isn't it?" he says as she weeps among the wreckage of her hopes for happiness with his friend Griffiths. "Fancy anyone wanting to be in love."

And who is to say for sure who is who? With our shrinks and our marriage counselors at our sides, the marriages of the seventies are crumbling all around us, while the marriages of the forties rise solid from the statistics. Maybe we expect too much not only of love but of marriage itself. Marriage is an honorable estate, but it is not nirvana. The marriages of the forties may have endured not only because society supported marriage but because the war generation expected to compromise occasionally. And did. Dr. Estelle Ramey, Georgetown University endocrinologist, once told a reporter in an interview, "Nature didn't really design us to spend a lifetime together. She was only interested in getting us together to bear children. The rest is up to us."

On the other hand, maybe the forties marriages endured

for the reasons Dr. Bowman advanced. Perhaps women, bringing fewer assets to marriage, did the compromising. I can't identify Louis Kaufman Anspacher other than that he was a speaker in 1934 before a Boston audience, but I admire what he had to say. "Marriage," he said, and maybe we could even add love, "is that relationship between man and woman in which the independence is equal, the dependence mutual, and the obligation reciprocal."

It's for sure we make adjustments and accommodations each according to our differing personalities. And sometimes what look like only mundane arrangements in reality run so deep and strong they defy words. I'm thinking of a farmer I know who runs a chicken stall at the market I frequent and who recently lost his wife of fifty years.

His weatherbeaten old face twitched slightly when I offered condolences.

"She never gave me no trouble," he said, making a minute adjustment in his row of roasters. "I guess in fifty years you kinda get used to each other. To each other's ways. I guess you could say it worked out."

I guess you could say it did.

Chapter

4

POSSLQs

Not long ago *Time* magazine announced that the sexual revolution, born of the affluent baby-boom generation and the freedom of the pill, is over, sapped by fear of herpes and by the general swinging of the pendulum back to a more sober way of life. Out are the singles bars, the one-night stand, swinging, open marriage, and constant focus on sex. Still in, however, is living together. It remains the normal pattern for the eighties in urban centers.

"Anyone with a modicum of attractiveness has two or three such relationships," says Desson Howe, a copy aide in his late twenties at the *Washington Post*. "All of us are probably looking to hook up with that one person, but if it doesn't happen right away . . ."

"It's absolutely the pattern," says Dr. Roy Nisenson, a psychoanalyist practicing in Westport, Connecticut, "except among religious groups who think of living together without marriage as sinful."

From the twenties right up to the geriatric set everybody's doing it, but the reasons why these arrangements exist are as varied as the people entering into them. The sociologists, psychologists, and psychiatrists are not in agreement about why, and indeed how can they be when the POSSLQs themselves haven't found out yet. About the only sure thing about living together without the license is that nobody gives you gift-wrapped Tiffany silver bowls engraved with your initials when you set up housekeeping without first visiting the minister. No wedding ring, no public commitment, no presents. The best you can hope for is some beat-up furniture not currently in use, lent by your mother, but don't count on it. The Census Bureau knocks at every door and inquires who lives within, who is married, and who is not, but their curiosity does not so far extend to asking if this marriage is an outgrowth of what earlier sociologists called "cohabiting." It is therefore anybody's guess how many marriages metamorphose from living together, how many POSSLQs ease on up to the altar. Some research points to about one in three, but the data is soft, and the reasons why some do and some don't are still in dispute.

"We're dealing here with a good deal of tentativeness and a very very frightened generation," says Dr. Nisenson, who sees in his practice a lot of people who made earlier mistakes. "Virtually everyone I see is divorced, remarried, or free-floating. People who were adolescent before 1968 and are now forty-plus frequently got divorced, and the options then were fewer. The women's movement hadn't come of age.

"Divorces hit people right in the pocket book. Living together allows them to discover intimacy without legal and economic terror. It carries tentativeness with safety."

Dr. Nisenson's patients may be forty-plus and solvent, but you don't have to be a battle-scarred veteran of a bum marriage to set up a living arrangement as a POSSLQ.

People now in their thirties came of age in the free-wheeling, angry sixties when the rule was never trust anyone over thirty, especially your materialistic parents. As students, they were the first to live in coed college dorms, and the first to whom the pill was readily available. They made

their own rules, one of which was Who Needs Marriage—
Take a Taste First.

Many a parent of the sixties generation discovered the new
arrangement when a voice of the wrong sex answered the
phone. "Are you giving a party?" they inquired innocently,
and the truth sank in gradually. The Vietnam war in its own
way changed the mores of the country in a manner, that ri-
vals, the aftermath of World War II.

With POSSLQs more than doubling since the early 70s,
the sociologists and psychologists have tried often to chart the
reasons, but the study of sexual arrangements is not a hard
science. High on the list and floating to the front as an explanation for hanging back from the altar is the prevalent failure
of marriage that men and women between the ages of twenty-
two and thirty-five see around them, especially their own
parents' marriages. If Mom and Dad are divorced or even
muddling unhappily along together, it takes much cautious
thinking before you tie a legal knot yourself. You have only
to look around to see what is documented in the Division of
Vital Statistics at the National Center of Health Statistics.
The projected rate of divorce for the marriages of the fifties
is 30 percent; in 1960, 39 percent; and in 1973, 50 percent.

Sometimes the POSSLQs have felt the fire firsthand. Dr.
Dennis Hogan, a sociologist at the Population Research Center of the University of Chicago, suggests almost one-third of
POSSLQs have emerged from divorce with a child, a fact that
tends to muddy the waters in a new connection, both economically and socially. Survivors of a broken marriage are in
a convalescent period, not yet ready to make decisions. And
they have economic burdens. Why not share expenses with a
steady sexual partner?

The new college graduates wore the most expensive com-
mencement hats yet, and many are personally paying off the
large college loans that made them possible. With the loans
coming relentlessly due and the job market in flux, who's
thinking of getting married when you can share living quarters, sex, and the food bill with no strings attached?

Who? Well, actually more people than first meet the eye. Tentative, cautious, gun shy, we still feel the imprint of the early unspoken messages of our parents, the imprint that was made, as Desson Howe says, "when our heads were soft, like the bound feet of Chinese women." Love and marriage haven't split for good. We women as POSSLQs have always had marriage in the back of our minds. Sex without marriage among women rose to a new peak in the '80s, but most of the time when we engage in sex we at least think we're in love. Marriage hasn't gone out of style. It's in women's heads all the time. It sneaks up on men.

Let me introduce you to Mark and Nancy Nicholson. Mark is a thirty-year-old nurse at Manhattan's St. Vincent's Hospital in the burn treatment wing.

"I never thought of marrying when I met Nancy," says Mark. "It was just date after date, and then it started hitting me over the head. In four months we were living together, and six months later I asked her to marry me. The indecision was kind of hanging over our heads, and it might have spoiled our relationship."

Did Nancy give any thought to marriage?

"Yeah, I guess so. I was twenty-seven, and I always assumed that when I got to be twenty-seven I'd get married. When it didn't happen that way, I got on with my life. But I thought about it early on when I met Mark.

"But I think my mother knew before I did. There'd always been boyfriends, but this was different."

"My own mother isn't living," says Mark, "but my surrogate mother kind of got into it and said if it's that way, why not go all the way?"

Mothers? This from the generation that examined their parents' values and, finding them wanting, discarded them. Mothers? Are we really growing up so that we feel that mothers are okay again?

"It had nothing to do with a desire for children," says Mark, and he's quite positive. "It was just a growing feeling that we wanted to marry."

They got married three years ago, live now in Greenwich Village and have a daughter, Lisa. Another child is expected. Nancy thinks she will work part-time after six-months' maternity leave from her work on a Ph.D. in biology. Mark works the 3 P.M. to 1 A.M. shift four days a week, so when Nancy leaves for the library, Lisa is in Mark's charge. Lisa and Mark are very close, and he's getting to be an expert in child care.

Mark and Nancy met at a party in New York, and she admits she had doubts about his profession. It was so different, how would it be? To put it bluntly, what would people think?

"But then right away I didn't care anymore," says Nancy. "I loved him and that was it."

The Nicholsons seem happy. Marriage is better than what they had before, they say. "I'm a lucky guy," says Mark.

"I really don't see why anyone marries," says the pretty young woman in blue jeans at the end of the sofa.

She's a POSSLQ. At twenty-eight it seems to be practically de rigueur to be a POSSLQ. Only seven years out of college, she's an editor on a famous newspaper supplement in New York. Her manner is diffident, almost shy, though professionally she's doing very well.

Her friend Kiki, who has brought her here, is silent. It seems to be up to me to defend marriage.

"Well, you know—kids," I say finally. "It seems to be nicer and neater to have it legal when you have children."

"Oh, kids," says Linda. "You mean to take care of you in your old age."

"Well, not exactly," I say. "Myself, it never occurred to me when I was having babies that I would ever grow old. The best I was hoping for was for them to grow old enough to get out of diapers."

"I'm not sure I want kids," she says. "They might upset the one-to-one relationship I have with Tom. Interfere with just the two of us."

I am beginning to feel like the last living survivor of the generation that took husbands.

"Oh, they will, they will," I tell her, "or rather, they would. A baby makes a difference. It's hard to be a twosome with pablum needing stirring and diapers needing changing."

Linda has an enchanting turned-up nose which she tilts slightly.

"It seems like such a waste," she says. "I've spent twenty-odd years polishing me. It seems wrong to devote all that time and then just raise babies. I could handle it, I know. I spent the whole first part of my life preparing for it. I was the oldest of seven. I was sixteen when the last was born."

Kiki stirs.

"You can be more adventuresome without a baby," she says. "Take risks, try things at lower salaries. Take chances. But every now and then this hormonal thing sweeps over me, and I have to get my hands on a baby. I have to go dig up a friend with children so I can pick one up. I think our generation is going to raise the godmother role to an art."

"They're not babies forever," I point out. "It's kind of a long-term commitment. Excuse the word."

"I'm afraid of what it would do to me and Tom," says Linda.

"It would be different," I say. "Is this the me generation speaking?"

She brushes this aside.

"My mother had seven, and she hasn't anything else now."

"With me it's a hormonal thing," says Kiki. "Maybe every four months or something."

It's funny about the parents of POSSLQs. Brought up in a world where sex, as least for women, mostly came after marriage, they are stout-hearted and learning the new customs fast. Probably sons are given into living arrangements a little more freely than daughters. POSSLQs are a fact of life over which parents have no control. Things happen little by little, and the message comes late in the game.

There is no support system for POSSLQ parents, as there is for parents of married children. POSSLQ parents rarely meet their opposite numbers. There is no surreptitious checkup on status or class, because more often than not these parents live in different cities and are known to each other only dimly through their children. Shotguns have gone out of style, and all-enveloping understanding is in. The eighties have uncorked situations for which there is no set of rules.

"I think my dad was a little embarrassed when he first met Ann's parents. You know, when they first came down to look over who she was living with."

Pete, who didn't want his last name used, is sitting on my sofa with Ann, on whose finger sparkles his grandmother's engagement ring. Pete looks at her, smiling gently behind his wrap-around dark glasses that do nothing to disguise the fact, evident to all, that he is clearly crazy about her. She is wearing her long blonde hair in two braids and her Nikes are muddy from their walk. Pete and Ann look slightly disheveled and very happy.

Two weeks ago Pete and Ann were POSSLQs. He's still not quite sure, in the fashion of his sex, how it all happened, how suddenly Ann is picking her bridesmaids and drawing up a list of wedding guests with his own mother. But he drifts with the tide, pleased.

"I thought we were just talking about marriage in general," he says, "and then one morning Ann said yes, she'd thought it over and she'd marry me. I didn't know I'd asked her."

"You've forgotten you asked me," Ann says, setting him straight with a smile that settles around him like warm sunshine. "He thinks *I* asked *him*," she tells me, and it's clear it's not a matter about which anyone much cares.

"Well, I love her," Pete admits finally, "so I suppose it's all right. It's a bit of a compromise, but it's a logical step. We like the same things, and the same things irritate us."

Ann had marriage in the back of her mind when she moved into Pete's apartment from her group house, which was not working very well, either the people or the setup. She works in an employment agency, and she moved in with Pete because his apartment was nicer. He's a computer whiz, one of the laid-back, slow-spoken, high-tech young experts born to microchips. ("I don't know what he's talking about," says his engineer father proudly.) At thirty-two Pete is seven years older than Ann, but it's easy to see she'll be the one to make the basic decisions and instruct him in their new life. "Just start the potatoes and cover them," she says on the phone when she has to work late. "Keep them low so they won't burn." He is learning fast.

Both sets of parents get along fine now. Pete phoned Ann's father to request Ann's hand in marriage, which must have touched her father, since the two had been shacked up for six months. Actually, her father cried at the news. Nothing personal, everyone is sure.

Living together was clearly a brief run-through of marriage. What took them so long?

Ann lets Pete field this question and we wait. Pete is never in any hurry with words and this takes longer then usual. When it comes, it's his generation's standard answer.

"I guess I went kinda slow because I saw my mom and dad having arguments. But I guess maybe everyone's parents do."

Pete's parents were married in the forties, one of those postwar weddings when the boys came home still wearing the uniform after saving the world, anxious to get on with love and life. One of those forties marriages that still cast their shadows on the children. Back when marriage was forever and differences were expected, differences that led to occasional discussions that left scars, but nothing like the scars of war. "We *expected* to compromise," says my friend Trudy, a college classmate still married after thirty-seven years. The message came through the headsets of their children: the natural order of things is love followed by marriage. The children of the sexual revolution filed it away, covered over by their own iconoclastic culture, like the subliminal messages on a TV screen.

"I guess I'm bigger on tradition than I thought," says Pete, crossing his blue-jeaned legs and downing the rest of his beer.

Ann will take his name. Like her mother before her, on the big day, she will shed her identity.

"He'd look like this if I didn't," she says, drawing in her chin and putting on a half-puzzled, half-disapproving look. Pete smiles, looking both proud and indulgent. Whatever Ann does pleases him.

"It will be interesting to see what the children of divorce today do," says Dr. Nisenson. "Children now about nine. History repeats itself, you know."

It may be like picking up a handful of sand on the beach and reporting that sand is dry, white, and coarse, but if the POSSLQs I met and talked to are a straw in the wind, they are mindful and protective of their parents' presumed inability to understand eighties sex customs. They do what they want, but they try to keep their parents from worrying.

Natalie Styker, a Chicago journalist, is a fine practitioner of the art of keeping parents ignorant of things that might disturb them. When her lover moved into her apartment, he did not answer the phone at hours Natalie's parents might call.

"My feeling for my parents has threaded through my whole life," explains Natalie. She loves them, you can see. She didn't want them to worry about their ewe lamb, now thirty-two, and a reporter on the *Chicago Sun-Times*, but grown, self-supporting woman that she is, she realized they would have trouble swallowing the news. Best they didn't know.

Nothing about this surprises me. I once typed stories about oil production on the IBM Selectric beside Natalie's. Natalie worried about her uncle who had lung trouble, about her aunt who might not adjust to the bad news about the prognosis, about her parents' planned vacation. Natalie understands cross-generational compromises and how life-styles don't translate well across thirty years' gap. Her family were in the dark about her live-in lover until she and he showed up in Seattle, and Joe went for a walk with her father to request his daughter's hand in marriage.

"But, Natalie, why did you eventually decide to get married?" Listen to what she says, and you'll hear once again the common denominator latent in every woman POSSLQ.

"Consciously or unconsciously, I had the feeling you got married when you fell in love," she says smiling. Natalie is a wow when she smiles. "We didn't discuss marriage at all until the night we decided to do it, nine months after he'd moved in. We talked it all out then and asked each other to marry. It was a big, big question. Both of us had been close to marriage before. But when we talked about it, it seemed so right that it was a matter of why not, not why."

After they got engaged, they bought a big house with a wrap-around porch and room for kids, penciled in in the near future. Natalie has always imagined a future with kids.

It sounds storybook perfect, but if Dr. Margaret Hall is right, only one of three living arrangements deepen into marriage. The stress that inevitably develops is harder to resolve when the final commitment is lacking.

"It doesn't turn into marriage," says Dr. Nisenson, "when one or both of the pair finally discovers who they are as opposed to who they think they are. When you live with someone, share meals and a bed, hear them go to the bathroom, they reveal themselves. But it's hard to identify why these couples don't marry because, even when asked directly, people don't care to remember previous connections that faded out."

"Actually they even forget [about earlier attachments]," says Dr. Dennis Hogan, sociologist at the Population Research Center of the University of Chicago. "This even goes for a former marriage. People tend to reconstruct their lives to fit their fancy."

On the other hand, shared living arrangements with people of the opposite sex can last as long as eight to ten years, says Dr. Nisenson, almost always in the high socioeconomic level where people pride themselves on being keepers of their own bodies without benefit of church, state, or societal approval. Often these couples have been married before and have discovered through therapy that what they are comes from within. They marry only to have a child. They like going places together, not because it's understood that they will but because they choose to. Their relationship is constantly renewed by their choice.

Beth Bogart, twenty-seven, a young public relations executive on her way up, is one of the people who stepped from a failed POSSLQ arrangement into another that ended in marriage. She still owns a house jointly with her first live-in lover, but it has all pretty well faded out of her thoughts since she is now married to someone else and is the mother of two. She says quite simply that she felt no guilt about the earlier venture; then or now; it wasn't the real thing. She felt no desire to marry the first time.

Then she met Desson Howe and quickly moved from a POSSLQ to a wife.

"I wanted a public celebration of a private joy," she says, "recognition that this magical fairy tale was lasting. I liked the sound of 'my husband' better than 'my boyfriend.' It was almost a subconscious desire for tribal ritual."

They arrived at their wedding, held in a bird sanctuary, in coach-and-four, possibly with the happy-ending fairy-tale symbol in mind. They bought an old house, with plumbing that couldn't pass the loan inspection, on the eastern shore of Chesapeake Bay, following up fairy tale with country idyll, as Desson puts it, and then, after discovering the grind of a hundred-mile round trip commute, a minuscule condominium in Washington, D.C.

"One lives with many people," says Desson, "and a lot

of relationships are purely experimental. But we grow up with married partners as parents, and we're programmed to think that's the way it is. Married is still what we expect to be."

Never underestimate those subliminal messages of youth. Desson, who grew up in a British boarding school and witnessed cruelty there and closer to home, says that he is the mother in his own marriage. "In a primeval way," he adds. "Short of breast feeding," says Desson, "I am the mother."

"It's true," says Beth. "He's made it possible for me to be a father. I've only seen a poopy diaper two or three times."

Of course, you've only just met these young people, and you may find it hard to understand this. You've heard of gender confusion, but this, by mutual consent, is gender reversal, all occurring quite logically and everybody content. You have to get to know them.

Beth is an only child of divorced parents, "a single jewel in a jewel box," Desson calls her. Her mother was ambitious for her. Born bright, she was encouraged to follow a script for success from the beginning, and she succeeded early.

"She's forward thrusting and she lacks the banal skills needed for calming down crying babies. Oh, she's the apple of her son's eye. He lights up when she walks into the room, but he knows that to tangle with me is foolish.

"The baby cries, and she sees grief in his tears, and it worries her as a double-jointed knee-jerk liberal. She translates her own child-oriented upbringing to him. What I see is a crying baby."

With a few personal real estate deals behind her and with ever more lucrative job offers Beth, even pregnant, was the breadwinner. She's recently taken a cut in salary in order to work for a more public-oriented firm, but she still far outearns her husband. He's not the slightest bit disturbed.

"Her income is by far the bigger," says Desson, "and I do not find it bothering. I'm not going to judge my value by the amount of money I make as a journalist. It could be ten thousand dollars or it could be one hundred ten thousand dollars in management, but that's not journalism. I was once intentionally unemployed seven or eight months working on my screenplays. We called it my D.C. grant.

"I'm not geared for [the pursuit of success], and Beth was groomed for it under a microscope. [Her parents] had a finger in every act. The script called for her to succeed."

You can hear the future arriving, as Peter Filene puts it, pointing out that machismo is disappearing in the middle class. It behooves us all to discard our stereotypes of husbands and think free about the new male. Filene says that even Hollywood has felt the breath of changing ideas. John Wayne is dead, he says, Superman giggles and blushes, and ET wants to go home. Only James Bond needs to take a sensitivity course.

"These are hard times for men," says Filene. If men are not to be macho, must they be wimps? Must a man be more like a woman? "Liberation," says Filene, "leaves man trapped between a rock and a soft place."

Things have gotten confusing, but in the end it may be a plus. If a man is freed of the macho image and of wimpdom, he is then, thinks Filene, free to have the best of both worlds. Free to bake bread and to play poker, to watch the Superbowl and also to bathe his children. He can wear hobnail boots and he can weep—mix and match according to his tastes with no disapproval from the culture. Gender conventions are disappearing.

I asked Beth if the role reversal bothered her at all. There was a small silence while she sorted out words.

"I resent it a little tiny bit. I suffer from it in little bursts of anger—why isn't he rich, why can't he take care of me? It's a teeny side of me that wants to be cared for instead of doing the taxes and bringing in more money and deciding what house to buy.

"But I'd probably go nuts with nothing to do."

I agree. Like Beth I figure my taxes and keep the books

and earn the living, and basically I'm proud of it. I too married a man who spared me at least many of the diapers and offered bottles to babies at inconvenient times. I was always handier with a screwdriver than Booth, and I changed the furnace filters. I still do. And what do I feel whan I ask a woman friend who her mechanic is or what kind of furnace she has and she smiles and says, "Oh, Henry takes care of those things." Outrage, that's what. I want to shout that women shouldn't abdicate on any ground, that life is uncertain, and it is every woman's duty to understand basics so that she is not a second-class citizen. And right after that, of course, I feel envy, if you must know the truth. Because deep down somewhere we women have a female streak that wants us to be taken care of.

Clearly, women POSSLQs are women with incomes, eighties women who understand how to handle money and probably landlords and garage mechanics, and often do. The possibility of their incomes exceeding that of their partners is quite real, as is the possibility of shifting understanding of whose chore is what, especially if somebody's child born of an earlier alliance is involved, as it is one-third of the time. No POSSLQ ever sat around knitting until the man of the house came home from work. In lower-income POSSLQ households, as Dr. Hall points out, there may be one job and one career, but in the more affluent arrangements POSSLQs are caught in all the conflicts of two careers and changing gender expectations.

And sometimes two apartments.

Bill Teltser, a New York City attorney in his early thirties, will tell you the apartment situation in New York was one of the two mundane things that combined with one he calls spiritual to change him from a POSSLQ into a husband.

Bill and Carol had been living together for several years in his apartment, squeezed by the difficulties of housing ceilings when, miracle of miracles, they found a larger apartment in the same building The new space allowed them to feel unhampered and relaxed and, in Bill's words, made it possible "to find a place in the world, lead a dignified life."

The second mundane thing that brought Bill and Carol to the altar was that Bill, who had been a labor lawyer in a high-powered firm in Manhattan, began to reassess his life and decided to go into business with his uncle in East Orange, New Jersey.

"I thought I'd try it for a year and see if it worked, and just as we got the apartment, the year I had allotted to try the new job expired, and I knew it would all work."

And what about the spiritual thing?

"It was psychological, potentially divisive. Carol probably cannot bring a child to term, and I wondered if at my age I could really tell whether I wanted a child and how relatively important it would be to me. And suddenly I realized that my relationship with Carol was the important thing. And it all came together."

And Carol?

"She's enormously wrapped up in her acting career, but I think she's not afraid to be dependent on a man. She doesn't find it demoralizing or defeating. I think if she'd wanted me to marry her before, she would have asked me. Now I see an opportunity to give her some emotional strength and support. You must understand this—you've been married."

Chalk one up for a relationship that deepened and matured with time as they sometimes do. Things sort themselves out eventually, one way or the other in POSSLQ-hood. Even when it doesn't work out, sometimes something good lingers. I have sometimes wondered what covered-over scars remain after a split, and now I see that sometimes they're not scars at all but only healed wounds. I learned it over after-dinner coffee at my friend Susan's house.

We are sitting contentedly watching Bob, the black lab—totally undemanding, as James Herriott once described all Labs to me—and waiting till it is time to go to a lecture. The men are scientists, friends of Susan's late husband, and they are discussing what must originally have been kept in the huge flask that sits near the fireplace. Underneath the discussion of rust solvents I ask the woman next to me if she has a daughter and, if so, has she ever been a POSSLQ.

The woman's expression is almost rueful when she tells me her daughter is breaking up a living arrangement of almost six years.

But why, I want to know, and as strangers on a train used to tell you their innermost secrets, knowing they would never see you again, she told me about her daughter's affair.

She was studying for her master's degree in Chicago when she met Henry, a surfer. "A what?" I inquire politely. I'd heard her correctly. And Henry fell in love with her daughter, though she had some small birth defects that had lowered her own assessment of herself and kept her from being the sweetheart of Sigma Chi and the cheerleader at the high school.

Caught up in her world, Henry became an academic himself and got his own master's degree, though before he fell in love he had not been much of a student. And when this woman's daughter moved to Los Angeles to teach, he followed, eventually doing a bit of teaching himself to keep afloat. Currently, he is working on his Ph.D.

He wanted to marry the daughter, but she was too busy getting her own doctor's degree, or maybe— her mother never said—she'd never really loved him enough to make it forever.

"So now," says my dinner companion, crossing good-looking legs and suppressing a sigh, "he tells her he's moving out. He wants to marry and there's another woman, but I don't know if that's the reason. All I know is that my daughter told him she wasn't ready to marry."

I stir my coffee and scratch Bob's back with my shoe and murmur that it seems rather too bad after so long.

The woman sitting beside me opens her eyes wide and shakes her head.

"Oh, no," she says. "Henry made a difference in her life, loving her, making her feel desirable. She's wrapped her work around her right now, but inside she feels good, I think. I didn't feel good about him at first, and her father was downright disapproving. You know, taking advantage of his only daughter. We were wrong."

Across the room they are still talking about solvents and reagents, and we lapse into silence, studying the fire.

I think about Henry and this woman's daughter and then say tentatively that maybe it is the man I should feel pity for. She smiles.

"Never underestimate the influence of a lover," she says finally. "He's no longer a beach bum, is he?"

And then it is time to go to the lecture.

What she said sticks in my mind. We don't give much thought to the current fashion; it's how it is. How are we to judge the fashion for POSSLQs until we can see it in perspective. And even then it will be hard, because what works out well for some is the kiss of death for others. We accept it and do not question.

But then I met Guy deCarlo, a vice president in marketing and sales, in a Poconos resort. A man "sixty, going on twenty-nine," a recent widower.

He's just had his first date as a widower with a woman in her late forties, perhaps early fifties. He called his twenty-two-year-old daughter, a POSSLQ, and told her. It was a step, after grief and loneliness.

"I'd love to meet her, Daddy," chirruped his daughter into the phone. "Bring her down here to meet us. We have an extra bedroom."

"Wait just one little moment," cried deCarlo into the phone. "One little moment. We're not shacking up. Isn't that what you call it? I hold her in very high esteem, but I'm an Old World Italian. We have courting periods. I'm not into your ways."

His daughter never missed a beat.

"Oh, okay, Daddy," she said cheerfully. DeCarlo has six children, and they respect him.

He thinks about this when he tells me.

"I perceive that we've passed the stage where all this is sacred ground," he says. "I told my children I wouldn't presume to advise them about such matters. You might as well try to hold back the tide, tell the wind not to blow. I introduce the man my daughter's living with as my pseudo-son-in-law.

"But," he says, "I tell my children that what they're giving away is of value to themselves. And after you've given that, there is nothing else to give. Then I say, you figure it out."

5

The Balance of Marriage

I never knew any of them, but the mothers of most of my friends have personalities in my mind. Ruth's was a Southern belle, cowed and twenty-three years younger than her husband. Sarah's mother was compliant, supportive, charming, and brave and was convinced that husbands were born boss. Tom's mother (rich in her own right) was an autocrat who dipped frequently into her son's life, armed of course with largesse as her credentials.

I know these women, all dead now, through the eyes of their children, and they left behind strong messages about the balance of power in marriage. Mostly they left their mark the way a road accident improves drivers who happen along later, but who knows for sure, because the molds of these women are not fashionable today. But what comes through clearly, is that the balance of these women's marriages stayed as they were their entire life long, with no amendments in the delicate unspoken agreement on territorial influence and power accepted by each before marriage.

In the eighties these tacit pacts are constantly subject to changed terms, partly because life keeps changing but mostly because we now accept that people do not stay the same. The women's movement made a gigantic difference, but so do personal crises and acts of God and the changing way we feel about ourselves and about the people we marry. Life alters us as we go along, and it hits us very unevenly. Some of us have to go to the movies to find out about death, infidelity, and disillusionment. Some of us get our noses rubbed in it, and we don't come out of the experience the same people. The better we deal with these things, the stronger we turn out. What breaks some toughens and changes others. Phyllis Rose, in her study of five Victorian marriages, *Parallel Lives*, points out that marriages don't go bad when love fades: "Love can modulate into affection without driving two people apart—but when the signals change about who is strong and who is weaker."

We are sitting on the floor in front of the fire, Joan and I and one of her classmates, sipping a postprandial cordial. I am defending myself because I changed my name when I married.

"I certainly wouldn't do it now," I assure them, anxious to be let back into the sisterhood.

They are tolerant, understanding. They want to find excuses for me.

"It was the cultural climate," Joan says kindly. She didn't know me in my tuna fish/mushroom soup/potato chip casserole days when I waited the day out until it was time to pick up Booth at the office. She didn't know me at the stage of my life when I spent my days shopping at Titchie-Goettinger for the exact kind of sheets and pillow cases I wanted and in Neiman-Marcus's junior department searching for a dress for afternoon bridge. I had quit my job fifteen hundred miles away and become a full-time Mrs. Mooney. My stationery said so, and so did my engraved calling cards.

Now I have two identities. One is the name in the phone book that cold-call brokers use to push a stock, and also furnace cleaners who want me to take advantage of their sensational offer. These people know me as Mrs. Booth Mooney because in big cities women living alone do not change the listing after their husbands die or they get nuisance calls accompanied by heavy breathing. Some of the chairmen of charity drives and the publishers of gift catalogs know me in this identity too. But if the voice on the phone is asking for Elizabeth, I listen. That's the me that counts, the me I became halfway through my thirty-one-year marriage, when I discovered that being somebody's wife and mother isn't enough. Now I know it isn't even a lifetime job.

When I went back to my typewriter, I had some small success, and Booth began to tell people at cocktail parties that he was proud of me. I have a little trouble with that phrasing now, but I didn't then, and we were both happy. My income was sporadic and never approached his, and he continued to pay the bills, as both of us accepted that he would when we married in 1946.

The balance had been disturbed, but the center was true.

And then he got sick, desperately sick, and couldn't work as he had before, and my modest cottage industry bought a badly needed refrigerator, a car, and new carpet for the stairs. Still he went on handing over the same check monthly, and I went on thinking of my income as auxiliary, buying pretties with it and taking fliers in speculative stocks. Texas men take care of their women, and he cashed in part of his life insurance and some stocks in order to hold up his role as provider. I signed our joint income tax without looking at his earnings, and when he died and at last I took a long cold hard look at the figures, I was stunned. His income since his illness was practically nonexistent. He hadn't wanted me to know.

I was stunned, but I understood. Right up to the end he was protecting me as best he could from unpleasant reality.

Maybe I couldn't have stood the truth in addition to his illness. Maybe I would have been terrified. We'll never know.

To this day I keep seeing him standing in a telephone booth, shaking with the aftereffects of radiation, as he makes one last try to set up an appointment for one more commission. He was a proud man and where he came from real men don't rely on women for support.

It's only now I realize the chagrin he must have felt at the last, when the phone would ring and they were asking not for him but me. I was just coming up as he, a one-man band swamped by illness, was foundering. He was generous to the last, shielding me from reality, rejoicing in my success.

The balance never wavered, though we were both becoming different people.

But that was in the seventies, in another generation, and Booth is dead, and people don't think this way much anymore. Today there are close to 50 million married couples, 47 percent of them both working. In 1981 three out of five married couples were two-income families. Generally, the women in the 1983 New York Times Poll we mentioned earlier said they found work and independence as satisfying as husbands, home, and children. At the same time Drs. Pepper Schwartz and Philip Blumstein, sociologists who conducted an eight-year study among couples across the nation, found it is the woman's job in two-income marriages that causes the most misunderstandings. More than four million wives earn more than their husbands. Look at those figures and you see that working women are the usual pattern in marriage.

It can't be—can it?—that young men coming of age when the women's movement has permanently changed the cultural thinking are having trouble with the idea of not being the breadwinner?

"I guess I think exactly as my mother did," says Debbie Johnson, who calls herself a workaholic, a typist/office manager in her mid-thirties. "I saw my mother treat my father as if he were head of the house, and I knew he wasn't. She was a government worker, and she made more than he did. She used to keep some apart."

It's a problem the marriage counselors see every day of their professional lives. You can listen to advice about it on the tapes available as a public service from various foundations and state-sponsored groups listed in the yellow pages. From the pressures of deciding who pays for what and who does what around the house come anger, injured ego, misunderstanding, and sometimes divorce.

"You see this misunderstanding of power roles most in the marriages of the late fifties, when men thought they were marrying sweet, sensitive, nonassertive women who then changed with the prevailing culture," says Phyllis Stern, a University of Maryland marriage counselor with a master's degree in psychology.

It may be more common in fifties marriages, but it's out there in all age groups. Debbie Johnson was a child in the late fifties, but she knows all about this. She even quit her job once because of it, though she's back at work now. Now it's all right, she says, because she and her husband are older. And he makes more than she does.

Debbie started her own business after the regular hours of her job at Comsat—Debtech Typing, technical typing she learned on the job and which she did after hours, with Comsat's permission, on one of their typewriters. Her husband, who worked at night the first ten years of their marriage, would bring the baby in his bassinet to her when he left for work.

"I made good money—five dollars a page—but it did something to the marriage," says Debbie. "The only time we saw each other was at twelve thirty A.M. I'd have a dinner prepared, but his nose was out of joint. He felt neglected, and I didn't have much enthusiasm for my wifely duties after midnight."

She made more money than he did, and she'd saved some from an earlier job. But then she just decided it wasn't worth it. She'd been in love with him since their first Communion, and she didn't want to throw any monkey wrenches into the marriage.

"He was like a child. I put these things on a scale, and it wasn't worth it. I quit."

She stayed home with her two children, following them around all day, picking up after them. Finally she took another job. And it's all right now. "He makes more than I do, and he's proud of my typing business. He tells people, 'My wife has her own business.' He's matured. He doesn't think he has to be the perfect daddy, the breadwinner. He likes the second salary now. He helps me. He's very positive. He shares the household duties."

More than a million husbands and wives both work and still cope with children under fourteen, according to two sociologists at the University of Maryland. Two paychecks earned on different shifts are especially common in the computer and health fields. What it does to the balance of marriage is still unexamined.

Unexamined but not unconsidered. The role of working wife and mother is having its effect on the face of America. Women now in their thirties are giving their daughters a very different role model from the one their own mothers offered, and it would be impossible for this not to affect the balance of a marriage. Respect and position came to women of the forties through their marriages. Their daughters are looking for something beyond the home and are raising their own daughters to see this as a given.

"Mother's father raised her to be a college professor. She was educated and intelligent, but she didn't become a professor. She had seven kids instead," says Dr. Elaine Swingle, a thirty-four-year-old Westfield, New Jersey, dentist. "When I told my mom I was going to dental school, she said, 'Don't forget your primary career for a secondary one.' "

Dr. Swingle, married to a thirty-two-year-old periodontist, has two children now and a busy, successful practice.

Her four-year-old daughter, Kate, knows mommies work and are doctors and thinks she might be a doctor too if she were a mommy. She told a reporter for *The New York Times* that if she were a daddy she'd do all the things mommies do.

Dr. David E. Nowicki, Dr. Swingle's husband, also does a lot of things mommies do in addition to his periodontal work. He gives his two young daughters breakfast, and he shares household responsibilities with his wife. Both his and his wife's parents were far more traditional in their household roles, and Elaine Swingle thinks that the balance of her marriage with David is closer to equal for this reason.

"When you work outside the home, you tend to share responsibilities, and things are more equal. Neither of us has any trouble with this. My husband has a very strong personality, and so do I. I think we tend to select partners who will understand our way of thinking. He knew when he chose me what I planned to do, and it doesn't bother him. He has a strong sense of self."

Everything in the end seems to depend on who the people involved are. It appears that younger and better-educated husbands have far less trouble with the prevailing trend toward working wives. Catherine Ross and John Mirowsky, University of Illinois sociologists, studied 680 couples, aged eighteen to sixty-five, across the country and concluded that husbands hold most of the authority in traditional marriages in which the woman does all the domestic work. This husband, says the team, is significantly happier than his wife.

When the woman works only because the couple needs money, neither partner is very happy about it, according to Mirowsky and Ross. She still is allotted most of the kitchen scut work. It is only in marriages of younger, better-educated partners, where women's work outside the home is more than an economic necessity, that the balance of shared chores was spread more evenly and the marriage is more of a partnership.

The team interviewed very few married partners in which

the husband made less than his wife, reflecting what Dr. Ross says is minuscule in national numbers. Earning power, she contends, is still a power base, and the bigger the gap the less equally household chores are shared. This was true even among the highly educated younger group, where the husband is more responsive to the cultural pressures on males to drop the macho image. Men on the track of advanced degrees may take the long view and be impervious to paycheck inferiority, but Dr. Ross thinks this is a special group.

But marriage counselors know there are other power bases beside the size of a paycheck to tilt the scale of a marriage. Whoever loves more is more vulnerable to the possibility of loss and is working under a disadvantage in a relationship or marriage. Sex is a power base, and nobody who reads the divorce cases in the newspapers will doubt that a fortress of power can also be built by annexing children or even in-laws. All kinds of unsigned, unwritten agreements, tacitly made and never acknowledged, hem us in, a lot of them made when we were different people.

Power, says Dr. Kyle Pruett, associate clinical professor of psychiatry on the faculty of Yale University, is a very complicated concept. "I don't think the sociologists have done a very good job of defining balance. What looks like power, looks like vulnerability, can be many things. Is it passivity? Sexual dominance? Intellectual dominance? Creative drive? All these things can make partners remarkably independent of each other."

Dr. Pruett has made a study of seventeen families in which the roles of nurturer and breadwinner were reversed. Husbands and wives ranged in age from nineteen to thirty-six and two-thirds decided on the arrangement before the child was born. None of these families considered itself different; they came to it because they needed the money and it seemed sensible, possibly because the mother had a job and the father didn't.

Dr. Pruett was interested not only in the children reared in such an arrangement but in what kind of men undertook this reverse role. In the course of interviewing them he found long shadows of the men's relations to their own fathers and sometimes to their mothers. Obviously, though the world changes around us, for better or worse we carry with us the stamp of our early childhood. "When I became a father I stopped feeling like a punk. It was like I was more my own father's equal," one nineteen-year-old told Dr. Pruett. One particularly devoted father-nurturer remembers, as others did, fathers missing, distant, or away a lot. The sons of these men were among the ones who chose early to assume the traditional mother role while their wives worked. Interestingly, as teenagers these men did not much think of fathers as nurturers but in terms of phallic pride in fertility and potency.

Growing up, the men were all either quite close to or quite distant from their fathers. They seemed, says Dr. Pruett, to marry women with independent aspirations who did not see their prime role in life as nurturing. He wonders if the androgynous family could be a three-generation flow of the psychodynamics of fathering, influenced by what Christopher Lasch calls our "age of narcissism." At any rate, he found these husbands a healthy heterogeneous group responding to a "compelling quartet of powerful people—mother, father, wife, and baby."

The weak sun is just struggling from behind a cloud when Juanita Koffie joins me at a table for two in John's Place. In the corner an elderly man nurses a cup of coffee as if he meant to make it last all day, and through the thin wall of the mall we can hear the *pow-pow* of the electronic games somebody is playing next door. Evenings clearly are when John's Place flowers. Now it is on hold.

Juanita is wearing the orange jacket of the Safeway checker. Her shift will be on duty in half an hour, and meanwhile we are planning to talk about husbands, and life when you're raising two kids on two salaries.

I have known Juanita for some time, but desultorily, no better than evolves from watching while she totes up my canned dog food, fresh broccoli, grapefruit, flour, and other necessitites of life. We chat while I count out the money. She knows that I am a widow, and I know that she has a new daughter and that this baby, Fatima, is her second. I didn't know that she had been married before, which she tells me now over her coffee.

She was only nineteen.

"He seemed so happy-go-lucky, and I wanted to escape my strict father. I was too young to—what's the word?—understand. He hadn't finished school, and I went with him to live with his mother in Virginia. I helped take care of his grandmother."

I thought about Bill Fripp and the law he wants to pass about not being allowed to marry under the age of thirty. But there was no rancor in her voice as she told me she hung onto this marriage for six years while he worked in the Newport News shipyards and an insurance company mailing room, and took a flier at draftsman's work. He turned unpredictable, she says, and she gave up, divorced him, and went to live with her sister.

Juanita has clearly learned to accept life as it is doled out. She gives me a little throwaway shrug. You can tell she thinks the mistake was hers, made before she knew what she was doing. She stirs her coffee thoughtfully and tells me she got a new job as a masker, covering rear vision mirrors and clock faces on new cars with tape to protect them in shipment. They promised her more money than they gave her, and when she complained, they said, "That's enough for a woman."

"They wouldn't dare say that now," she says, and we glower together, angry that they could ever have said it.

She quit and went to work for Safeway. She wouldn't give her present husband, Tono, her telephone number for a whole year. Four years later she married him.

"It's more quiet, this marriage," she says with the peculiar accepting smile that is part of her charm. "I'm not rocking the way I was before. I'm content.

"He's African, and in African culture men get to name the children. I said, okay, give me a list of names, and I'll pick from there. Fatima was the only one I liked. Now we've renamed her Dede—first-born daughter."

Tono has a fleet of taxis, his own business. He's ambitious, she says, and you can see this is a relief after the first fiasco. He's thirty-five and already has twenty cabs. And a second daughter, named Koko, whose middle name is Lynice.

"I gave her the second name," says Juanita.

"At first he made all the decisions, but now it's different. Really different. I say, no way. Hold it."

In Africa women don't get to name their own daughters, but let's not be uppity. Only young working wives in America hold equal power in the domestic setup, and even this is not an iron-clad rule. Women now in their fifties and sixties submerged their lives completely in their husbands' when they married, and many still do. The wife without a paycheck will not call the shots, and though she may get very adept at influencing decisions, she will not decide where she and her husband will live, whether they can afford a new car or a vacation home. She will say who they invite to dinner and she will choose the friends. Call her first vice-president in charge of social details.

I was lunching with some women, all of whom married in the forties, and during a pause in the conversation I asked the pretty widow beside me if she had completely submerged herself in her husband when she married. I know her as a busy interior decorator with a talent for sprucing up a room that makes me respectful. She holds a good job in an uptown business firm from which she would like to retire, but her employers resist losing her.

"Oh, yes," she says with a smile to melt the heart of an IRS auditor. "It was my pleasure. I loved my husband."

Then her smile fades, and she remembers the night before the funeral when she was having a cup of tea in the kitchen with her sons, trying to accept the fact that she was widowed and sole captain of the ship.

"We never had words in front of the children," she tells me. "There weren't any disagreements that our sons knew of. He was a good husband. And I'm sipping my tea, and my older son reaches over and puts his hand on my arm and says, 'Mom, now you're free.' "

Next time your're tempted to write off children as unaware of undercurrents, of the give-and-take of their parents' relationships, remember that son comforting his mother with a gentle reminder that a wider life awaited her.

It's not right, of course, to lay it all at men's doors. I know a man who had a fine job with a future if he would relocate on the West Coast. But he had fallen in love with a woman who had no intention of leaving the East and the small town where she had lived all her life. She was the village belle, she was happy there, and who knows what she'd have been elsewhere? He married her and turned down the job. He didn't go west. Not, that is, until years later when life had rewritten the script and all kinds of balances changed. Then he went without her.

That's a thirties scenario played out by the last generation—to see women as comfortable to come home to, keepers of the hearth. Since then we've had such a cultural upheaval that husbands have been known to pick up and follow a wife who has angled a better job in another city. I have friends who for years had two homes, one in Philadelphia and one in Washington, in which they spent alternate weekends together, married and employed in different locales, working the week separately in his and her cities. "We're in Washington this weekend," Frank would call and say cheerfully. "Come for a drink."

"It's a completely different world than our fathers knew," says Rick Porter, a thirty-nine-year-old math professor at Brown University in Rhode Island. "We're all with some difficulty coming to grips with the fact that we're not God in the household anymore."

Rick got an intensive bath in the contemporary woman's perception of herself during his first marriage, when he was a graduate student at Yale and his wife was a fellow academic. Whereas his work was moving right along, hers was not going well, which, according to him, she had trouble accepting. The resulting friction killed the marriage. "You like to think you're going to do something with your life, and you want to get on with it." He couldn't stand the trauma kicked up by his wife's perceived lack of direction.

"This who-am-I business finally became unacceptable," he says. He is married now to a woman completely absorbed in their children from earlier marriages, working part-time teaching small children in order to educate her own in private schools.

"Who's in charge?" I ask him. "Who makes the decisions?"

"We work them out together," he says comfortably, and his wife, Mary, nods. It's clearly a working arrangement, a new balance born of what each has discovered through mistakes before they knew what they really wanted. They're not in competition in the world of academics.

One thing we know for certain is that the women's movement does not speak for all women, and I don't refer here to followers of Phyllis Schafly. Listen to the radio talk shows and you'll hear the waves of disapproval aimed at working women with small children from mothers at home with the kids. Eavesdrop at any gathering of the wives of affluent men in their fifties and sixties and you'll find very few ripples of uneasiness over the balance of marriage. Older women admire in other women the attributes that do not denigrate the role of housewife. "She's so pretty," I heard one woman say, "and it turned out she had a high-powered job, but you'd never have known it. You'd expect her to exchange a recipe." For these women's daughters, careers are understood. For themselves it is understood that husbands work and wives make their homes pleasant. If it ain't broke, don't fix it. Everybody's happy.

Still, by and large, it looks as if both women and men are taking women more seriously, approvingly or disapprovingly, and the result is a lot of mental gymnastics, reshuffling of partners, and adjustments on everybody's part. How you feel about it depends on who you are and how you spend your time, but how men relate to women has been altered across the board. The current ideas get tossed around in bars, shadows of them flicker from the TV and movie screens and scream from the covers of the women's magazines, become the theme of the decade for novels, and make appearances in the comics—Cathy may be the new folk heroine. But they're all filtered through personal prejudice and experience, and some unusual scenarios are required for adjustment.

Men are reassessing, struggling to be what the new culture demands—the New Man, newly programmed to the requirements of the eighties woman.

"I'm not sure what a man is supposed to be," says Jules Feiffer's cartoon man. "Do I share? Do I care? Do I feel? Do I give? Take? Grab? Am I compassionate? Passionate? Cool? Cold? Vulnerable? Am I sensitive? Am I normal? What's manly? What time is it? I'm going back to bed."

"I'll have to call back in a minute," says Debbie Johnson. "My daughter's at the beautician's and I don't know if she's ready to come home."

When she calls back, she wants me to know how she has worked out the inevitable strain of trying to make things perfect under the pressure of two jobs and two children.

"It all started," she says, "after my second was born. My pressure was up—Miss Perfectionist, you know. I went to the doctor. He looked at me and he tested this and that and he didn't say anything for a moment, just reached into his pocket. He got out a hundred dollars—he was a family friend—and he told me that was for running away from home."

She didn't think much of the idea at first, but she went home and cleaned the house as if it were spring cleaning time, and cooked up a storm and put the results in the freezer. Then she took the children to her mother-in-law and checked into the Ramada Inn twenty minutes away. Her mother-in-law knew where she was, but her husband was only told Debbie had to get away.

"The first time I did it I took an article of his clothing with me. All this time his friends kept saying to him, 'How do you know she's alone?' I guess they worried him, but he trusts me now, and I do it two or three times a year. I just need to get away."

I feel pretty good thinking about Debbie and her marriage and also about that loyal mother-in-law, and over the phone, before her daughter needs to come home from the beautician, I tell her so and wish her luck. I would have told her that her husband is a lucky man, but there wasn't time.

She laughs and rings off.

"Wish me patience and rest," she says.

Stumbling through difficulties has brought many marriages to a more even balance, with traditional roles altered and adjusted to changing facts. Men have felt the change in the climate and adapted their thinking. Nobody cares to be thought out of date; it's the wrong image in the eighties.

But there's one thing they'll never change and that's buried deep in women, something atavistic that's common to us all. We don't like looking down on our men. Level is okay; looking up is better. We all know that, and marriages that don't make this possible are starting with built-in risk. A woman marrying for money can at least tell herself that, even if he acts like a wimp, he had to be smart to earn all those lovely dollars. Or maybe to have been born of aristocratic and well-heeled parents. But somewhere along the way things might get off the track. And she may well, as life goes along, get her come-uppance in another setting.

There are variations on the theme. Maybe she didn't look down on him, but she was the dominant personality, and he, maybe because he didn't care or was a peaceful sort, doesn't do battle. Everything rocks along just as long as no testing of shaky foundations takes place, and then, *pow*, another hand is dealt and it all falls apart.

Frances Hofnaegle tells me she loved her husband, and I believe her because she doesn't fool herself and therefore her friends and acquaintances. Nevertheless, when she married him, she was already a recognized authority on education and had no intention of retiring into the role of housewife. The year was 1931, and she made an unusual covenant with her husband that he would never object to her continuing to work and would be willing to hire enough servants so that, even though she did not run the house, they would live in comfort. "My money," she told me, "was understood to be available for Hardy Amies suits. And other nice things." She held an important job, and the kids, when they came along, were puzzled to learn at school that other mothers stayed home with their children.

With territorial division clearly marked out, things went along splendidly, and there were very few conflicts. "Oh, disagreements, yes," says Frances. "The servants, I remember, were always forgetting to water the new trees, and I thought he should tend to that. But I think really he was proud of me and my carreer."

Now flick the pages of the calendar up to 1972. Frances's first husband is dead and she has married again. She and her new husband live in an old Pennsylvania farmhouse in exurbia, and both are retired. But the balance is different. Ralph, her new husband, doesn't drink and doesn't go with the girls who do. So Frances, the former woman ahead of her time, never takes a drink in his presence, though out of his sight she enjoys a snort.

Why does the woman who walked on little spike heels through the corridors of power so much of her life, laying down game rules at home, suddenly turn pliant?

She doesn't say anything for a moment or two, and I wonder if she has never asked herself before.

"I would have been lonesome without him," she says finally. "It would be too late to look for another. He was my anchor."

You notice she says "was." They've parted. You can think about that from all kinds of angles.

And then there's Julia, Kiki's mother.

Julia is one of my close friends. It's funny what makes people friends, lifts them out of the list of acquaintances, raised into confidants. I knew Julia because our daughters were friends, but then I knew a lot of people that way. I can pinpoint the moment when I knew Julia and I would be friends. It was in a seedy gas station in the wrong part of town, into which she had limped with Kiki and Joan when something went wrong with the mysteries under the hood. Summoned, I transferred the little girls to my car and wished her luck as I wheeled off toward the school. In my rear-vision mirror I saw her shrug her shoulder and spread her arms, palms open, speaking volumes about the perfidies of the world and the necessity of accepting the blows thereof.

We fell in love with Chinese food together, and over lamb with oyster sauce and kung pao chicken our friendship waxed. Books we consulted about, and food, and kids. Her pursuits were sendentary.

It was a dozen years later that she phoned to say she was bringing over lunch from the deli "because I have something to tell you." So we sat on my tiny back patio and devoured sticky rice, basil beef, and pickled cucumbers, and I knew before she told me that she was getting a divorce.

"But how did you know?" she demanded, mouth agape.

People, of course, always assume that their friends notice nothing as marriages disintegrate piece by piece.

We skipped that one, and then I got the news that I hadn't foreseen, that after thirty-five years of marriage she would be trying again. "A skier," she said with her mouth full of rice, looking ecstatic. "We have already bought a house. Two miles walk from the village."

"Walk?" I cried in disbelief. "You're not a walker. Your idea of nice afternoon is a nap in the down comforter and the *New York Times*."

"I'm going to start walking. I'm going to enjoy it," she said, grinning.

And suddenly I believed in this marriage with a husband I had never met. And in the remarkable capacity of women to change their thinking to please the men they love.

But not for one minute in the projected walks.

Couples marrying today expect that women will have life-long careers, according to Arthur Norton, assistant chief of the population division of the Census Bureau. It's understood. The rub comes most often when her income exceeds his and his ego damaged. But in this, as in most things, it matters how a person feels about himself.

There's a male voice that answers sometimes, or used to, when I called Joan at the Family Studies office of Catholic University where she once worked. I'm inclined to call her from time to time to ask her opinions on life or if she has found her watch or if she has tried a restaurant I'm thinking of going to. The answering voices grew familiar, and I got to know the people, sort of like long-distance friends passing the time of day.

Jack Lewis, a twenty-eight-year-old graduate student whose dissertation will be finished next year, is one of those voices. He's been married less than a year, and his wife, also twenty-eight, is a microbiologist earning three times what Jack earns. At present Jack's a house-husband, but it doesn't bother him one whit.

"It doesn't make any difference," says Jack. "I'm a little self-conscious about it, but I like being a house-husband. I like to cook. I've taken a fancy to it. Marian works sixty hours a week, and I kind of like to do the day-to-day stuff."

How does Marian feel about this?

"She wants to get a maid," says Jack. "There's a cleaning woman where she works, and she could come once a month. I guess I'm a bit disillusioned. I like putting on records and scrubbing away together, but I know she'd much rather go for a ride in the country or a walk in the park."

No, they didn't have any agreement about duties and money before they married. It was more like kismet, with no forethought. They met, lived together six months, and a year later married.

"It was more a naive type of arrangement—no forethought. My friends were sort of surprised it was so quick," says Jack.

He's a different man than before he met Marian at a party at his group house.

"Being single has its pleasures, but one of the differences between me now and single is that all that going to serious movies, sitting around and talking about the tragedy of life in dark bars late at night is alluring, but at a certain point in your life you don't want it anymore. I guess you close off part of your life when you marry."

Well, obviously Jack is secure enough not to worry about male angst in the midst of new patterns, but what about his friends? Are they confused about what's expected of them?

He gives this his usual intelligent, serious attention and answers that the talk is overblown. He thinks women are confused too, and it'll all work out.

"I don't think it's all that different from when my dad married in 1940. He lost twenty-five pounds in a month worrying about it."

Gracious. Why?

"Well, his mother-in-law, my grandmother, is an unusual person."

While I'm swallowing this, he tells me that his father and he are closer than before he married.

"You know, I think it's pretty much the way it used to be. Maybe we dream different dreams, but the same old things worry us—where to live, money, children. When I hear all this talk about the new pace, the difficulties, the balance, I start to wonder, is this guy happy in his marriage? In 1940 life was pretty fast too, with the war. My father and I talk about it."

Marian, oh Marian, you lucky woman.

Chapter

6

The Husband
as Father

Complete role reversal like that in the Desson Howe family is probably rare, but there is no getting around the fact that the prospect or the reality of a child has a profound effect on a relationship between two people, married or not. Bill Teiltser wondered if it would make a difference later. Desson embraced fatherhood in a way that would leave an earlier generation open-mouthed. And to Jessica Whyte, heavily into an important relationship, a child was the breakup wedge. When the man she was living with made it clear that he was totally disinclined to be a father, she finally understood that their values were too different for them to stay together.

The culture takes strange bends and twists, and what yesterday was the rule is out today precisely because parents observed the rule. "In Olden Days a glimpse of stocking was looked on as something shocking, but now Lord knows, anything goes," wrote Cole Porter in the 1930s. Each generation asserts its right to rewrite society's rules. But reject as we may, the way we were brought up affects our basic thinking. The harder we rebel, the deeper and more resistant to uprooting lies the early programming. And though the family has had hard sledding lately, fragmented by corporate priorities, total sexual freedom, and the restlessness of America, most of us grew up in families we felt good about and that left us with values that remain.

Ask Jessica Whyte, who loved a man who didn't want to be a father.

Whyte, who is in her mid-thirties now, tracked a path of rebellion in her early days that must have few equals. Product of a well-to-do Richmond Virginia, family, she had what she calls now "the rich girl syndrome." And for a while she laid her guilt complex for her fortunate lot at her parents' door.

"I didn't feel my parents knew me at all," she says. "They didn't give me coping mechanisms, and I held them responsible for the inequities of life. I had all these things, but I was only born to them. My father was with Nixon at the time, and I was pretty sensitive about it."

She was supposed to be a shoo-in at Vassar, from which her mother and elder sister had been graduated, but she was not. She went instead to Wheaton.

"I came home for the summer, and my parents said, 'How are things at school, dear?' 'Fine, but I'm not going back.' I dropped out and went out to teach the Navahos.

"Up until then I had led a sheltered life. I found that the Navahos hated whites, even those trying to help. I was exposed for the first time to real poverty, and I felt hated for reasons beyond my control."

It was a downward spiral from there, with a period in California with someone she now calls "a street kid." After a while she was heavily into heroin, and her parents, in desperation, urged her to enroll in Second Genesis, an organization that helps people break addictions.

"It was very black and white to me at that point," she says now. "I had come close to running. It was a suicide road, and I saw what they were suggesting was my only clear chance. I took it."

They did a good job at Second Genesis. They helped her. She quit drugs and found a job, a secretarial job, even though she had been studying for a master's degree in education in California, having finished her B.A. at the University of Pennsylvania. Because Second Genesis understands that reentry is difficult, she lived for the first three months at the home. At the job she met Kip.

"I was infatuated from the jump start," she says. "He was living with a group, but we took a house together. I was still pondering dope, and I needed acceptance and he gave it to me. He gave me wonderful support on a rational level. But on some level I felt he was holding back emotionally."

She began to think of a child, but he said from the beginning he didn't want one. But they stayed together, shoving their differences under the covers, avoiding clear conflict. His mother came to visit and thought it was all wonderful. But Whyte had trouble dealing with it. "I have a very clear notion of commitment to family, and on a rational level it was okay, but emotionally it wasn't right," she says.

But they had bought the house together, and in her heart of hearts she convinced herself that it would be all right, that perhaps it is impossible to find all things in one man. And then he went out and got a vasectomy.

The operation is not always completely effective for the first four months, and for three of these Whyte used no birth control. But then it sank in on her that this was for real and that her values and Kip's were miles apart. She left him.

"I was passed on a commitment to the life force," says Whyte. "I was almost born with it. I place high values on family."

Whyte herself is the first to say that this is not necessarily a trend. Only one of her friends, she says, feels as strongly. Martin O'Connell, chief of the fertility statistics branch of the Census Bureau was quoted in *The Wall Street Journal* recently pooh-poohing the idea of a second postwar baby boom. But if there isn't going to be an overwhelming number of babies, it's possible the ones produced by this generation of high-salaried executives are going to be taken seriously by mothers and fathers alike. No longer is a father a remote figure to an infant.

It begins now with prenatal classes with the father-to-be in attendance. They graduate right along with wives, stand by in the delivery room, and often rise without complaint for the 2 A.M. feeding. Today's fathers know things about babies that would cause their own fathers to blanch. I wouldn't be surprised if today's fathers knew things I still don't after having been the principal figure in three births.

Fathers appearing in the delivery room is an idea undreamed of in the fifties. My own husband, hearing that I was experiencing premature labor contractions, called an ambulance and slammed the door on my recumbent figure. "Aren't you coming?" I quavered. He had, to my knowledge, made three practice runs to the hospital. "I haven't had my breakfast," he shouted, waving cheerily, and it says less about our marriage than about the era that I didn't think to reply, "Neither have I." I had the baby alone in the hospital corridor, attended only by a man summoned by my cries for help from his post-hemorrhoid operation bed of pain. He took one horrified look and staggered down the corridor in search of a doctor.

Today it's a whole new ball game. I know a man who is so delighted with his brand-new son that he recently skipped lunch to meet his wife at the pediatrician's office to get a report straight from the doctor's mouth on the baby's progress.

This baby, I will say, was longed and hoped for eight years before his arrival, which occurred only after uncounted visits to fertility specialists. But the baby's grandmother also experienced some delay in getting pregnant, and his grandfather never saw the inside of a pediatrician's office. Parenthood, excusing biology, has become close to a partnership.

Last time I passed through a gynecologist's office almost half the chairs in the waiting room were occupied by men.

Lots of these men had their noses deep in magazines named *Baby Talk* and *Your New Baby*. The office of Dr. Robert McDowell, a pediatrician in the capital, reports that more and more fathers are bringing infants for their checkups, though this slacks off after the first few months. A similar story comes out of Cambridge, Massachusetts, and other cities across the country.

If these fathers are like thirty-seven-year-old Randy Kingman of Gaithersburg, Maryland, it isn't that they are not heavily involved in their work. It's more that they are beginning to realize that early childhood, once missed, is gone forever.

"I think I love my work about as much as anyone I know, but I've had to reassess my priorities," Kingman says. "I guess I see now that in the long run I'll be judged less on my contributions as sales manager than by what kind of children I have. Being a father has changed from when I was the child, and it was a mother's job for ten years, and then fathers came in to wrap it up."

Kingman's wife, Karen, is a teacher at the college level and is deeply involved in her career. Like Randy, she's thirty-seven and thinks her friends who married late will see more of this attitude than she did when she had her first baby thirteen years ago.

"Randy's a good father," she says, "but until lately he's been more involved in the fun stuff: 'Let's leave this mess in the kitchen and go to the circus.' "

"I'm suddenly realizing that Allen is thirteen and Laura ten and adolescence is just about here," says Randy. "Then they won't care who I am. They'll want me to butt out, and I'd better develop credits now."

Jonathan Cummings, a thirty-three-year-old Washington lawyer whose wife is also a lawyer, isn't worried much about how the world would judge him if he left care of their two children to her, but he would judge himself harshly. Washington lawyers know no time clocks, and both work a better than eleven-hour day, counting traveling time to their respective offices. They have so little time together that it is almost axiomatic that both share it as a matter of course with the children.

"It's a closer marriage than if one partner had all the care of the children and the housework as well," says Cummings. "Sharing removes a potential source of friction that might arise in a marriage where the work is more divided—the grass is greener sort of thing." Neither of these lawyers on the way up gets home before 7:30 P.M. as a rule. They have hired an au pair girl, but it's Cummings's wife, Ann, who gets the meals. They sit down nightly somewhere around 9 P.M., spelling each other holding the eight-month-old baby. It's a bit of a juggling act that is truly shared.

And what about household chores, the laundry—that domestic albatross—the dishes, the rest?

Cummings, who doesn't blanch at diapers, doesn't feel household chores are demeaning either. "Just boring." He says he doesn't have a high level of requirement for neatness in the nest and consequently doesn't notice things that exceed Ann's toleration level. Which means she does more of the work than he does. "But I try to carve out my own niches by fixing things," he says. "I think biologically and sociologically women are more programmed to nest keeping."

The demands of a career and the difficulty of managing a demanding job for fifty to sixty hours a week have kept many women from having children at all. Four out of five of a group of women, all with the title of vice president in firms with annual sales of $100 million or more and who have no children, say they don't regret the decision, according to a recent joint Wall Street Gallup Organization survey. Fifty-two percent of the women interviewed are childless. Of those under forty, with time running out for a change of heart, only 36 percent have opted for motherhood.

Is this because motherhood would be spreading them too thin? The survey didn't ask, but it did inquire of the mothers among them if husbands were pitching in to help. Yes, they said, the chores were pretty well shared.

Except the laundry. Laundry was the one chore husbands of female executives did not pretend to share. Randy Kingman was right in style when he said, "I try to be there for my children and always have, but my disdain for doing laundry hasn't mitigated one tiny bit." Yet with Mummy stretched superthin between job and family, it would have to be Superwoman who doesn't get tired and cross occasionally and demand more understanding of what's required. A full quarter of the female executives in the survey felt they had succeeded, at least partially, at the expense of their husbands.

Still, not all working mothers have vice-president on the door, and if you ask Dr. William Baxter of the Marriage and Family Institute in Washington, D.C., women are not, despite all the sound and furor, as involved in their jobs as men are. He suggests there is something in the biological makeup of women that makes it easier for them than for their husbands to divide their attention between job and kids. Although Dr. Baxter draws his experience from an upper-middle-class group of husbands and wives who seek professional counseling, he thinks often the woman's job is aimed at providing a summer home for the family or to enhance the already adequate income of the husband.

And as political polls do, he thinks sociological studies influence people's thinking.

"If a wife reads that 98 percent of men are getting more involved in the care of children, she feels men should get more involved. I think mostly the guys are pretty reasonable and work out a good balance. I hear from the sociological studies that there's a major change in father involvement, but I mistrust this.

"You don't change cultural patterns overnight, and they frequently snap back. What we're seeing is a modification of the way it was."

But what certainly has changed is the way working mothers look at their homes.

"Frank used to call me late in the day and say 'get a sitter and join me at the club,' " says the mother of three working daughters, all with children. "How could I get a sitter with no notice? I couldn't go, and I'd resent it after being home all day with babies."

Her daughters want nothing more than to get home to their children after a ten-hour day at work. Beating their husbands home is devoutly to be desired and changing a diaper looks almost like recreation to both after a day with high-power career demands.

But it isn't only in two-salary households that the question of father involvement comes up today. Elizabeth Joplin, a thirty-eight year-old Philadelphian married to a lawyer who is the sole breadwinner, says that when her son was born two years ago, Ken, her second husband, was by her side in the delivery room, though he never considered such a thing when his daughter by an earlier marriage was born.

"It was strange," says Elizabeth, whose friends call her, for no reason that anyone can explain, Biffie. "He doesn't do diapers because he says he feels squeamish about them, but he felt he'd be all right at the delivery. None of this picture-taking stuff, recording the event, but strictly for support up at my end and not the doctor's. He did fine. And it mattered to me too. That couldn't possibly have happened in my first marriage.

"But I have to say Ken likes babies. My first husband didn't feel comfortable with them. I have pictures of him with the two boys, and his whole expression says, 'Awk, what is this?' Now we have an au pair girl, but if we didn't, Ken would be very good with little Ken.

"All but the diapers."

Pause.

"I don't know what makes him think *I'm* especially equipped to deal with diapers."

Biffie, who has a strong sense of self, doesn't think work-ing wives have more reason to expect father involvement than full-time mothers. At thirty-eight she just missed being born into the world of predominantly employed women and does not feel apologetic.

"I don't need a job for identity," she says. "I was at a wedding not long ago and sat at the reception with one of the partner's wives who is an attorney too and the mother of a two-and-a-half-year-old. She kept saying how hectic her life was, and I kept thinking, well then, why does she do it? She certainly doesn't need the money. I wouldn't *let* my life be hectic."

She does it by choice, we both agree, as does the father who goes into the delivery room and the one who devotes part of his Saturday to giving his infant son a bath. The au pair girl today is the Mary Poppins of the two-salary household. Armies of British nanny services stand ready to take over do-mestic chores, day care centers proliferate, some even at the work place. Two professionals can buy what their parents, unless they were rich, never dreamed of—competent full-time help. A father today can, if he wants to, to be as remote from his small children as his father was from him.

But often he is not, and if this turns out to be a trend and not just a blip in the cultural pattern, it may be the best thing that has happened to America in a long while.

Because my mother was an invalid I was raised as a small child by a succession of nurses, God-fearing Irish ladies whose business in life was taking care of other people's children. They got me into my smocked gingham dresses in the morning, and sewed up my teddy bear's seams when they split, and took me to Sunday school and birthday parties. If I showed signs of getting out of hand, they threatened to quit, which was the furthest thing from their minds but terrorized me be-cause I knew my father depended on them. They wore won-derful black hats skewed through with hatpins when they went to church on Sunday, and they earned a decent living for the time rocking in the front porch wicker chairs while I read and put puzzles together.

But it was my father who dominated my childhood. A covey of these women waited on him, cooked the meals, and stayed with me when he was at work and at parties in the evening. But I always knew that, whether he was at that mysterious place called the office, on the golf course, or dining at one of my courtesy aunties' tables, we were a duo. In his free time he sought me out and talked to me, not down to me, adult to child, but gravely as if I were his equal. Sitting beside him while the shoe-shine boy at the Smoke Shop buffed his shoes, standing beside him at the post office window while Mr. Curtis sold him stamps, helping him select the freshest vegetables at the market, I was completely happy. He told me how his maiden sister annoyed him and how he felt when he caught the huge trout mounted over our sideboard; he complained to me that he hated the little dishes the cook served the vegetables in.

He took me for after-dinner drives around the lake, my legs stuck straight out in front of me on the seat, and pointed out the blue heron standing stiff and silent in the shallows, looking solemn and benign as a preacher in a pulpit. He confided that he had caught his yard foreman in a lie, and that was stupid because truth fits truth the world over and a damn lie fits nowhere. He warned me that no one would ever learn to play good golf who didn't swing from the inside out. None of this was earthshaking, but what came through to me was that I mattered to him.

I loved him extravagantly, and I carry something of him with me still, though he is gone nearly thirty years.

And this, of course, is quite different stuff from giving small babies bottles and baths, but who is to know; perhaps they're cut from the same cloth.

Chapter

7

Husbands Who Don't Want to be Husbands Anymore

We're driving up a long alley of trees arching gracefully over a driveway, a long beautiful approach to a country house near Baltimore. We are here, Joan and I, to lunch with my friend Julia, who has lived in this house for twenty-plus years with her husband, Al, and their two children.

"This," I say to Joan as I avoid a Maryland mud turtle ponderously making his way across our path, "is one of three truly happy marriages I know. You know, actively happy, not just having got used to each other and made allowances."

"Um," says Joan, drinking in the countryside. Joan, who lives in a city house, loves rural delights.

We were late, which I hate to be, and Julia was standing in the door when we rounded the circular drive approach.

"I was worried," she says as we put our arms around each other. We have been friends a long time, since Joan was a basket baby and neither of Julia's children were yet born.

"You're thin," I say into her ear. "Have you been sick?"

"I'll tell you at lunch," she says. "Here's Al."

More hugs all around. Al wasn't coming to lunch. He had to see the man about the sheep he rented to keep the grass cut. Even exurbia has grass problems. He would give me a ride in his new pickup truck when we came back. Rides like a limousine, he promised, and the price going up $200 Monday. He might buy two. We waved good-bye, tooling out the long alleé, talking about Joan's job, the cutworms on the tomatoes, about nothing.

Julia told us about it at lunch. About how Al had come down the stairs one morning, pronounced the coffee just right, eaten his egg, folded his newspaper, and announced that after twenty-nine years he wanted a divorce. There was this younger woman, a friend of their children really, and he wanted out.

She shook a little when she told the story. The fried potato skins came and went and nobody could touch them. Divorce papers had been filed, and shortly she would move to an apartment. Oh, and she had been the last to know. People had kept the news from her, protected her.

Why do men do this?

"They're afraid of losing their vitality," says Dr. Nisenson, "and if they can satisfy and be satisfied by a younger women, they feel renewed, more able to cheat death. Women get screwed because they submerge emotional and professional development for years in the needs of husbands who are out in the world exposed to vital people who stimulate them. The wife has no energy left to develop herself, and in the end the man feels she bores him."

The doctor is right. You hear it every day.

"George doesn't think he's going to die," says a happily married friend of mine. "He won't mark birthdays. Men are afraid of aging. Women are more in touch with the realities, maybe because they have the babies."

I am angry for Julia and for all the other Julias out there who are fighting against a limitless supply of younger women stretching into infinity. It's a no-win game with weighted stakes and simply illustrates the fact that is not generally acknowledged: women are different animals from men, realists who admit the basics. You hardly ever meet a woman who thinks that in the matter of aging an exception will be made in her case.

Katharine Hepburn, that remarkable seventy-four-year-old who has never suffered accepted notions gladly, was quoted once in *The Wall Street Journal* as knuckling under to the idea that biology is destiny.

"Sex," she says, "is an irresistible force created by the Almighty to populate the world, and when a woman passes her child-bearing years she becomes less desirable. A man of sixty is apt to marry a much younger woman, and a woman doesn't have that choice unless, of course, she wants to pick up some dumbbell."

All of this is true, but sometimes there isn't a younger woman in the offing, or any woman at all.

I'm thinking of, among others, Eleanor Link.

In my college photo album Eleanor sits with her long legs tucked under her, holding a big bouquet of field flowers, one hand on the crown of a huge cartwheel hat, smiling into the camera. I think I remember we were amusing ourselves with photos a la Vogue, six Smith freshmen on a summer vacation in Maine with not much to do. She was prettier than most of us, but everybody's nice to look at at eighteen and we were all eighteen. In my photo album we are all forever eighteen. Eleanor got married, as we all did, and has grown children now, but she's one of the not too exclusive company of women whose husbands wanted out of a long-term marriage. The woman he decided to make his second wife was ten years younger than Eleanor, but fifty-eight and forty-eight aren't all that different. "I'm going to have one wild fling before I die," he said. (Hear the intimations of mortality?) He and his new love were married and Eleanor is divorced.

Happiness is never guaranteed, but the worst pain is inflicted by someone you love. It happened six years ago and it still hurts.

"I put my arms around my daughter to tell her the news," says Eleanor, "and she said 'I feel like killing someone.' "

He was a lawyer and handsome.

"All his clients noticed that, I'm sure," says Eleanor, "but I felt secure. He seemed to prefer me. It was a real shocker. She was one of his clients, and he'd only known her three months."

There has to be a difference between the way men and women think, though I suppose a lawyer might back me into a corner, shaking his finger at me and saying sternly, "What you mean is there a difference between the way Eleanor and her divorced husband think." I accept that, but I'm unconvinced. It's more often, I think, that men miss the impact of what they consider a reasonable request than the other way round. Women just have keener antennae for receiving emotional wavelengths. Witness this scene set in the early stages of Eleanor's divorce.

Her husband had just moved to his own apartment, awaiting the divorce decree so that he could remarry. About seven o'clock he called Eleanor just as she was preparing to sit down to her solitary dinner. It was clear to her from the clinking of ice and the gay laughter in the background that he had guests for cocktails. "I'm just calling to find out how you make that good chicken thing with the mushrooms and white wine," he said cheerily.

He was obviously astonished, says Eleanor, when she replied tartly that he should ask his intended. "The recipes go with the lady," she said. She wonders about his insensitivity still. "Didn't he have any picture of me sitting down with my dinner at the same old familiar table in that 'melancholy little house we built to be so gay in.' That was the phrase that kept ringing through my head. I think it comes from Browning's

'Andrea del Sarto,' and I used to find it haunting in college, probably prophetically."

There were other things, "each one astonishing me with the realization that he had simply no idea of the huge and awful hurt. Or what the whole thing was all about. He always cried at movies. I'm sure if he had seen it all in a Bergmann film he would have wept his eyes out for the pain of it all."

But why do husbands do this? Let's leave *how* they do it for the moment for *why* they do it at all. Is it really true, as some biologists have said, that the desire for variety in the male is nature's design useful in primitive societies for impregnating many females and not really curbed in industrialized society?

"My theory is male menopause," says Eleanor. "You know, lawyers lead very sheltered lives, surrounded by adulation. He was a superb attorney, but I think he felt he hadn't contributed enough.

"His whole life is different now," says Eleanor. "I don't think I'd have cared as much if it had been someone just like me only better. He was the dirty sneakers, Maine type, and now he's on his fourth Mercedes and goes to gallery openings.

"I feel lonely as hell, and I keep gnawing it back and forth still. There's anger when I talk to him about the children and, not like a widow, I know somewhere, he's alive and not sharing our children and grandchildren.

"Maybe it all has to do with the me generation that rubbed off on ours.

"I don't know. God knows I've thought about it."

Dr. Hall thinks that divorce instigated by men who have been married twenty to thirty years is due to the fact that men are simply less attuned to handling midlife crises by adjusting than are women. "Women, with their habit of introspection, their nurturing skills, are more sensitive to the quality of relationships. Men opt to shift arrangements while women examine and adjust."

Daniel J. Levinson, professor of psychology in the department of psychiatry at Yale University, in his book, *The Seasons of a Man's Life,* calls the years roughly between forty and forty-five in a man the midlife transition period during which he enters middle adulthood. He and a team of researchers examined the lives of forty men in various walks of life, and he now views this period as a bridge between early and middle adulthood, when men must review their lives and reappraise, test new choices, and deal with "polarities [which are] sources of deep division in his life." This is a difficult period because by now most men have made choices that have given them a set structure even as he hears within him voices of "an identity prematurely rejected, of a love lost or not pursued."

In his book Dr. Levinson says that dealing with his own mortality means a man must engage in "mourning for the dying self of youth so that the self can be made whole again. To do this, he must experience some degree of crisis and despair. No single event marks the end of early adulthood as puberty marks the shift from childhood to adolescence." A change of partners, a younger woman, can mark the transition splendidly.

Dr. Levinson points out that a man's life structure evolves through orderly sequences of stability and transition. The stable periods last six or seven years, ten at the most. Then come the transition periods in which he reexamines early choices in a new light. This period may be marked by drastic changes, "a change of job or occupation, a divorce or love affair, a serious illness, the death of a loved one, a move to a new locale." If there is no conspicuous change, there may be a more subtle one, a change in the relationship to his wife, for instance. He sometimes feels a sense of defeat, that his life has not accomplished what he hoped. This is the period during which "with the fog of illusion gone, he sees his wife as a person." He may even recognize that, for him, the marriage was flawed from the beginning, that he married for reasons no longer paramount to him. He is able to do this, says Dr. Levinson, because he is now capable of dealing with his own illusions about himself. He sees that he and his wife have developed in different directions.

Dr. Levinson studied only the lives of men, but what happens to men ultimately affects women. Let me introduce you to Catherine Sensinger, a California woman whose husband, in his early forties, reappraised their marriage of more than fifteen years and chose to marry a younger woman. Fifteen years later Catherine looks at herself in that period with unusually clear eyes and paints a picture of the collapse of a marriage brought down by what seems to be just such a mid-life transitional period.

Catherine met her husband at graduate school. She'd just emerged from a traumatic time following the birth of an illegitimate child, whom she put up for adoption, not being able to cope with the responsibilities of motherhood without a husband. Until then she had thought of herself as an independent woman who had been through a period of rebellion, but overnight she reverted to a period of craving dependence, a pattern she thinks now was there all along. Biologically and psychologically she was ready for marriage, and at twenty-five she married Fred, then twenty-seven, "probably for the wrong reasons."

"He superimposed on me his ideas, as later he superimposed new ones on his new wife. Meanwhile I put myself under his umbrella, watched his parade, and robbed myself of my own identity. He had a strong image of his heroic role with women."

When this marriage ended, her husband suggested that she, he, and his new love live together in a menage à trois. He figured that Catherine would grow to love his mistress as he did. It would not, of course, be quite what his colleagues and his maiden aunts in North Dakota would understand, so he proposed to marry the new love to give the children a name and Catherine could live right next door. "He wanted," says Catherine, "what men traditionally want, controlled polygamy," an arrangement she compared to the eighteenth-century French upper-class ideas.

"He was very serious," she says, "and surprised when I told him it was totally impossible. He was ordinarily clever at making things happen."

So how did she come to terms with Fred's new choices and the division in her life?

You get the impression when you talk to Catherine Sensinger that you are talking to a capable, strong woman, reciting a story she read somewhere else. But she says it wasn't like that.

"I was bruised after the divorce, still licking my wounds, hurt and bleeding, but now the psychological need for leaning is over. The sex side is less and less important to me; I hardly think of it anymore. I suppose I still entertain the fantasy illusion that someone who is very right for me is out there, but less and less. I'm not hungry; I'm not sending out signals."

She's living now with her twenty-eight-year-old daughter with whom she shares a deep bond. She knows it will be hard when the daughter leaves, but her journalistic work is very engrossing, very exciting to her. She'll manage.

There we are, the essential, fundamental difference between men and women. You'll find plenty ready to say that women of the World War II generation stopped growing when they married, but these women were bright, resourceful, interesting. The mistake they made was to focus their lives on men who moved on.

You hear the same story replayed at ever level, every age group, variations on the theme. Natalie Neviaser was more than ten years younger than her husband, and there wasn't even another woman. She didn't have any idea anything was in the wind until she heard him calling a divorce lawyer. They'd been married twenty-seven years, and she had encouraged and trusted him, handing over her paycheck from a government job regularly, downplaying that it was bigger than his from the postal service. When he departed her life, she didn't even know where their joint savings account was.

He was a letter carrier with a posh route in the suburbs, and when he retired the people whose mail he delivered gave him a party. The paper sent photographers. Natalie thinks that he couldn't handle retirement.

"He never told me, but I gathered he tried to get part-time work and couldn't," says Natalie. "We stayed under the same roof until the divorce was final, and I left the house only to go to my job. My job saved me. I kept thinking how I had encouraged him to go to night school and get his college degree."

Twenty, thirty-year old marriages date back to the fifties and sixties with a divorce rate projected on the basis of statistics ranges for, say 1965, from 26.9 percent to 43.7 percent projected, with nearly 30 percent already crumbled as of seven years ago. That leaves a lot of marriages currently in one piece probably stumbling toward dissolution—people now masquerading as reasonably content, going out as couples to friends' houses, sharing a double bed and an established routine, the third act of the scenario yet to be written in final form.

But statistics are misleading, says Jim McCarthy, demographer at Johns Hopkins University. He's wondering about the popular conception that men consistently marry younger women the second time around. There are more remarriages than divorces reported, and that can't be. Something's wrong somewhere. Telephone surveys are conducted by household, and the person who answers the phone may not know the answers or may be biased. It's possible that men remarry more quickly than women, but nobody is sure. "Men lie more," says McCarthy.

Whatever the vital statistics, there's feeling in the wind that men cheat more in marriage. Karen Richards, mother of two, a Washington housewife in her late thirties, says many of her friends' marriages suffer from cheating.

Her close friend Becky went to the hospital for an appendectomy and returned home to recuperate. Feeling better, she followed her doctor's orders to walk a few steps each day and rose from her bed to get a cigarette. There in the living room, assuming she was safely immobile, were her husband and another woman engaged in sex on the floor.

"It devastated her," says Karen. "She still can't talk about it except to me, but she says the pain was worse than the appendicitis. She divorced him and she's married to someone else now, but it lingers in her mind after three years. I suppose it was the male menopause again."

Cynthia Doyle is a twenty-eight-year-old lawyer whose company sends her on the road to conferences in other cities. Hospitality rooms, wine and cheese hours follow business, and Cynthia sees a lot of contractors, twenty-five to forty years old, who mingle socially after hours.

She is single and they mostly are husbands.

"They're constantly on the make," she says. "I guess I was naive. I didn't understand that men wearing wedding rings consider themselves totally free away from home."

Propositioned for a one-night stand, she eyed his ring and inquired sweetly, "Are you going to tell your wife about this when you get home?"

"Why should I make her unhappy?" he says, offering Cynthia another glass of wine.

"Maybe she has a boyfriend?"

"No. It doesn't work that way. She wouldn't do that. We have three children."

Cynthia went to bed with a report, shocked. She was angry because she was attracted to him.

Shocked? In the eighties? Open marriages have been around for some time.

"This wasn't open marriage. This was unequal standards."

It is possible that men and women want different things from marriage?

"Let's guess and say that years ago a man married more from a need for comfort, moving from his mother's house to his wife, with each caring for him as he worked. The needs of men and women today coalesce more than that, though still skewed toward women doing more chores," says Dr. Nisenson.

That's as good an answer as any to a complicated question, depending, of course, on who you are and when you marry. But even today the joy surrounding an engagement announcement is tilted toward the bride-to-be, a reflection of our culture's belief that marriage still offers more of the things desirable to women than to men. He is caught; she is chosen.

Sure, we both are looking for that one-to-one understanding and closeness that makes everyone else a bystander. But women's needs are more complex; we give it more thought. Will he *always* love us, make a good father for the kids, fight the world if necessary in our behalf? Still understanding of course the new concept of equality in domestic labor? Will he love me tender?

And men? They're probably looking for the support and softness the business world does not offer them. And to move on from the competitive singles scene, maybe even hoping for a hot meal at the end of the day after the sales meeting, with all the caring welcome that implies. But they don't formulate these things in their minds. These ideas occur to them later, when the woman who might provide them crosses their path. Men probably come to marriage with fewer preconceived expectations.

But what makes a man want to abandon his marriage?

To begin with, divorce is no longer considered a disgrace or even a failure but, in the idiom of the culture, an opportunity for personal growth. In other words, no big deal.

When I was growing up in Rome, New York, divorce was considered a matter for slightly raised eyebrows. Divorcees were thought to be "fast" and therefore rather interesting to men. One of my mother's friends was divorced, and only the most secure of the Romans invited her to dinner. She didn't come with a man and thus clearly could be on the prowl.

She had met one of the well-fixed local couples on a cruise, and on impulse, since she seemed to be amusing and in flux, they suggested she settle in Rome. She did, bringing her son, and her shipboard acquaintances sponsored her until she was admitted to the closed circles of the town, the country and the city club. She was widely admired for her crisp, direct manner and fashionable clothes. She dyed her hair, the town whispered, probably with red ink, but such fun, really, and witty. She captivated the town's bachelor doctor who lived with his maiden sister, and the two of them became a regular duo at the clubs.

She had no money, but she had flair, and she entertained without servants, serving things like chili and other dishes foreign to the cooks of Mother's friends. She was breezy and outspoken, just what they all expected in a divorcée. But she made the mistake divorcees are reputed to make: she wooed the doctor from his comfortable relationship with a prominent widow who had been one of her staunchest supporters, and the town closed ranks.

It is said there was a face-to-face confrontation, a showdown between the ladies, both of whom were in their sixties or closing in on them fast but no less emotional than they had once been. Gifts that had been given were returned, hard words spoken. The divorcee was no longer seen at the club and soon was missing from fashionable dinner parties. The doctor solved the problem by dying, but the ladies remained unfriendly and the rift was left unhealed. The polite shunning continued; people chose sides and few favored the divorcée. I can still see my father shaking his head in amusement. "And all over Oliver," he would say, grinning. "I think he wears a corset."

The picture of the divorcée common barely twenty-five years ago—selfish, irresponsible, and shady—has been altered barely within the last twenty-five years, as Margaret Mead pointed out. The change is recent, but it's complete; even the Roman Catholic church is less unalterably opposed to divorce. When I married in 1946, the Episcopal church refused to allow the wedding to take place in church because of Booth's divorce, and I had to be married at home, which deeply worried my father who feared the floors would collapse under the weight of the guests and had them shored up with braces in the cellar. Today a divorce is a rite of passage, and our first divorced president sits in the Oval Office. So what else is new?

The things we expect from marriage are of course constantly changing with the culture, and our disillusionment with how it might have been is altering as well. Originally, it was clear to every female with half a brain that her status and security in life depended on the man she married. You could start out as a secretary and leapfrog over the backs of a dozen better-paid people by getting a ring on your finger. Brains just got in the way. To win a lifetime income with no trouble you needed only a certain amount of feminine charm, a focus, and the opportunity.

A majority of women relied on marriage for economic security, and if you botched the job, you had only yourself to blame. There weren't many other options unless your daddy provided your security. The movies spun it all out in fairy tales of love and marriage; girl meets boy who is apparently poor but turns out to be the boss's son working his way up from the bottom. The message was everywhere. Educate the homely daughters and let the others marry a wage earner.

So there is a whole generation out there totally reliant on

the earning power of the men they married, making them into para-children, dependents. The danger, according to Barbara Ehrenreich in her book *The Hearts of Men: The American Dreams and the Flight from Commitment*, is that "there is no guarantee that a man's emotional dependence on his wife will last as long as her financial dependence on him." Ehrenreich goes on to say that the last generation has been born that will make the bargain of financial support for caretaking, but the fallout from these bargains is still with us. Jean Cheney Spock, former wife of the famous pediatrician, Dr. Benjamin Spock, has founded a support group in New York City for women over fifty-five who have been dumped. She herself was divorced at sixty-eight.

Many women must fight for a place in the sun, but if you don't have to worry about that, will you try as hard to make a marriage work, compromise a bit even though you can walk away from a breakup financially independent?

"Women do, they still do," says Karen Richards. "My mother's generation had to accept that bargain. I earn the living, you do the scut work. We don't, but still I see my women friends trying to be flexible about who does what, responsibilities, peculiarities. I don't think *men* have changed much from my father's day."

Her friends who married "too young" feel they have missed something, says Karen. Where were the hot tubs, the swinging singles discos, when they were having babies, holding down crummy jobs to make ends meet instead of climbing up the career ladder? And the singles of today? In the 1983 NBC documentary examining singles and marriage in which interviewees across the country appeared, only the women were thinking of vows at the altar. The male interviewees, gazing sincerely at the sociologists in their trendy beards and sweaters, looked gleefully happy to be unencumbered and free to sample what is offered.

It's difficult, except in a general way, to find out from a man the root cause and the final difficulty that ultimately shattered his marriage. If there was commitment in the beginning, pain has filled that void, and men, being slow to articulate pain, emotional trauma, or anything to do with their personal life, seldom speak of it. Not one word did my husband, the most articulate of men, utter about the thirteen years of his previous marriage.

I was introduced to his first wife once or twice before the divorce, but I knew nothing of her, barely knew her name. The closest Booth, a careful man with words, ever came to shedding any light on his marital past was a fierce look he gave me once as we sat in a restaurant awaiting dessert.

"Never serve me cooked bananas, will you?" he said suddenly, and his voice was loaded with such emotion I was left to imagine the whole thing had foundered on bananas.

I never inquired how things went wrong, honoring his silence. I don't know to this day.

My friend Harry's divorce took place after the children were grown and married and was very sudden. We talked often after he became divorced, were thrown together as the unmatched people of life are thrown together, but still he never referred to his new status though it was implicit in his bachelorhood, which paired us off. The furniture was split up, his wife remarried, but still no word on the subject passed his lips. Rugs disappeared from the floor, he sat alone at his dining room table, and still the subject stuck in his throat. One day we talked on the phone for ten minutes about inconsequentials, and when I hung up I considered for a moment and called him back.

"I am aware that you're divorced, Harry" I said. "You know you're divorced, even if you never mention it. We both know it. If I can help, I will. Let me know."

He seemed touched, but the divorce remained a taboo subject between us, like a withered arm, even after two cocktails.

The pain, of course, varies with the love that died, but if you have not seen the wreck occur, the ashes of a marriage will likely remain untouchable if you rely on a man for confidences. All you can be sure of is that it's easier for a man to avoid examining why's. Root causes might trigger unpleasant thoughts, and the less attention given to the whole thing, now over, the better.

"Tell me about your husband," says the man sitting on my sofa, a man I last saw in 1942 when he was a fighter pilot and I a cub reporter. "Or don't you want to?" Mike is always thoughtful of other people's feelings.

Mike never met Booth. He was overseas shooting Germans when Booth was P.R. at the army base in Rome, and when he came back, we lost track. I married and he married, and our worlds diverged so that we didn't meet again—until forty-two years later when he picked up the phone, having run into someone who knew where I was.

I told him about Booth. I told him how we borrowed $200 to go on the honeymoon, and how my father disapproved because of the divorce, how Booth had died suddenly in my arms on the kitchen floor.

Then it was Mike's turn.

His first wife died sometime ago, and he married again, a marriage lasting five months. He had told me about that when he first phoned, and he had laughed when he told me, a laugh, I thought, at himself and his five-month mistake.

I hadn't pursued it then, but I did now. I wanted to know about his miserable five-month failure.

"What went wrong?" I asked him, and I wasn't worried about treading on treacherous ground, remembering the laugh. But now, on the spot, he fell silent.

"What was missing?" I persisted. I couldn't square this quick bust-up with what he had told me earlier. "You have to work at marriage," he had said, and maybe you do; I don't know, though I'm far more inclined to believe that good marriages are a matter of dumb luck and timing.

Still, it stuck in his throat, and an uncomfortable silence fell. When he finally answered, he skipped over the words so that I didn't understand him and had to ask him what he'd said.

"Love and affection," he said and fell silent. I had asked and he had thrown me a crumb and kept the rest close, but I was ashamed to pry further and we left it there. I still don't know whose love and affection was missing, his, hers, or both.

You can, of course, sit next to a stranger on an airplane and learn, against your will, more than you can stomach about his ex and his messy divorce and his opinion of women in general. Which only goes to prove that pain comes in different packages, and often there is no pain at all, only relief, and even something like elation. Or that strangers will tell you anything. The demographers will never package it, capture it in their charts and statistics.

For three days, on and off, Mike and I tried to fill in the missing years of our lives, and as we drove to the airport, were still trying. We were both in our early twenties when we first met in the club car of the Commodore Vanderbilt, steaming up the Hudson from New York City, and in the way people did then, because it was wartime and the country was one big family, we scraped acquaintance. "Along about Herkimer," he says, quite positively. I think I remember that I was the scraper, but the moment is gone from my memory.

He moved into another lane of traffic, as we both considered how it was then.

"What would you do different if you had a second chance?" he asks me, and I knew he wasn't talking about that train.

"Nothing. You?"

"Spend more time with my children." Then he said something that stuck in my mind. "A man's ego is far more fragile than a woman's. We have a hard time too. I think women have lost something."

I studied his profile and the good tweeds and London Fog covering up a fragile ego. I never noticed insecurity in the men in my family, and it was hard for me to believe I was looking at one now. But down at the Marriage and Family

Institute, Dr. William Baxter, minister/consultant, who has sat in on some fourteen thousand group sessions of troubled men and women examining split relationships, has thought about it and heard about it.

"Man's ego is based on sexuality, affirmed and confirmed," says Dr. Baxter. "Men are more like little boys than women are like little girls. Men thrive on approval and like to be in control."

There I am, in the passenger seat of my own car, wondering if Mike has made a veiled comment on my lack of feminine softness or a general complaint about the culture and his own adjustment to it. This is a man of sixty-five, part of a generation of men who took care of their women, lit their cigarettes, opened doors for them, put on their overshoes, and brought home their paychecks to them. And I, having once had all those things done for me, have moved on to fight my own battles, cope with recalcitrant plumbing and roof gutters and faulty furnaces, deal with incompetent garage mechanics and unreasonable employers, and face the fact that the best things in life may be free, but while you're not looking, they get snatched from you. I am now only looking over my shoulder at those days. For better or worse, like millions of other women I've learned to rely on myself, and there's no turning back the clock.

The women's movement didn't do this to me. Life did.

"The irony of the male/female relationship is that when men are young they deny need," says Dr. Baxter. "Marriage decisions are tough for them because they look on them as giving up their freedom. Women's needs come earlier in life, a need for security, for nest building. Men's need for tenderness comes only as they age, while women as they grow older become stronger, better able to handle life."

The voice on the phone is deeper than I remember, but I know it well. It's Eleanor, who has thought about our earlier conversation and wants to add to it. She wants to tell me about her psychiatrist to whom she went for two years to learn to live with the fact of a husband who didn't want to be married to her anymore.

"The shrink kept telling me to send out vibes, messages that I was receptive to dating. And I kept telling him that I wanted to be *me*. What if I don't want to send out vibes? Any woman can create a climate that flatters a man enough so that he takes an interest in her. But do I want to?"

She walked out of the psychiatrist's office forever the day he asked her if she'd ever considered a facelift. It sounded, she said, and her voice was still angry, as if he hadn't been listening all this time.

Women seem to learn more from divorce than men do and are certainly less inclined to shovel it all under the rug and prop up an RIP sign when a husband has departed. They may discount warning vibes at the time, but they can pluck them out of their minds later to examine what happened, what went wrong and where, and they're not afraid to. They'll shake out every fold of the marital disaster and usually can point to the moment when the thing was past fixing. Lauren Reddy, a twice-divorced woman of forty-one, now a lawyer, can look back and circle the trouble as easily as a play doctor studying the script of a Broadway flop.

She thinks back over it quite dispassionately, and when she comes to the bad part, she sloughs it off with an amused laugh, implying that it no longer matters, but you're not entirely sure. It's a quicksilver laugh, and it says she's smarter now, but you think it may have mattered a good deal earlier.

She can pinpoint the problem. It's what men and women separately want from marriage.

"We want intimacy," she says, and she's quite positive. "Best friends, the total thing. And men find that difficult."

She met her first husband while she was in college pursuing an advanced degree because she had not yet met the man she wanted to marry. But she married this man and followed him to a job in another city, merging her identity into his, teaching to add to their income, and setting aside her own work on a doctorate.

She worked and he worked, and finally there was enough money for her to quit and finish her dissertation. But she got a divorce instead.

She laughs here, a laugh for the unsophisticated academic studying bugs who thought she had found the answers. Now she knows that she's only just begun to understand what the problem was.

"Success was the major part of my husband's life. I came after success and so did my son. First, last, and always his mind was on success. He was cold. Talking to him now is like listening to a speech."

He was a lawyer, but he used that as a tool to get bigger things. Their son had problems, but he had no time to help straighten him out.

"It was up to me. '*You* go to family counseling. Send him out to the experts. Get him fixed. *I'll* pay the bills.' "

But why didn't she complain, demand he take his mind off the career climb and put it momentarily on the boy?

"Oh, communication wasn't our problem. I complained. We'd talk about it at cross-purposes and we'd never get anywhere."

The divorce left her shaken and with a bad self-image, even though, being attractive, she was dating several men. She was beset with what she calls now free-floating anxiety and continued to be for a year.

"I was very fond of him," she says, and this time she doesn't laugh.

So after a while she married again, this time a man who had been married several times before but who had plenty of time for her and took her around the world and to gallery openings and first nights. She stayed married to him five years, a record for him. Then she got her second divorce and enrolled in law school.

"A bunch of my friends took me to lunch to try to persuade me I was crazy. But I took the law boards the next morning." Now she lives with her twelve-year-old daughter, and after two marital crack-ups the law is coolly satisfying.

What did she learn along the way?

"That men suffer from boredom," she says at once. "They think changing partners will do it."

Though there are plenty of men in her life now, none interests her.

"Older men like to wear women on their arm. It's just not interesting. Now when I go out, I feel I'm wearing a mask. I have to remind myself to smile, react."

Is it the differing expectations of the sexes, the unalterable differences?

"That's too simple. Men have problems too."

What is there in a man's makeup that makes him so prone to get up in the morning one day, gaze into the mirror, and demand of himself, "Is this all?" Facelifts, hair dye, aerobic exercise classes—we women embrace them all in our fight against the calendar, but we don't fool ourselves; we're only trying to put the best face on what we know is inevitable. In men the inevitable seems to undermine the very foundations of their self-image. Let me loose to live my life, they cry, before it's too late.

I was mulling this over when the phone rang. It was Liz, a college friend of Joan's, who somewhere along the way got to be my friend too. The thirty-five years between us get lost somewhere when we talk to each other.

It never surprises her when I move directly into cosmic questions. I know scores of people I can talk to about what flicks we have seen and the new restaurants in town, but with

Liz, a lawyer on her way up, I can talk about the things that matter. She puts her second trunk line on hold and considers the matter.

Today I am seeking her opinion on the essential differences between the sexes.

"Do men shy from marriage early on because they're afraid of the burden of responsibilities?" I ask her.

"Sure. What else do you need to know?"

I cradle the phone comfortably between shoulder and ear and think.

"And women your age are more eager to marry than men the same age?"

"I think so. I don't suppose anyone can say for sure, but yes."

"Do *we* ever look at the responsibilities of marriage as a possible burden? After all, they fall pretty heavily on us."

She doesn't hesitate a second.

"No more of a burden than life," she says. "The inner office is buzzing. I have to go."

Chapter

8

*Picking up
the Pieces*

They bring covered dishes and sympathy to people who have been widowed, and maybe they should do the same for the newly divorced. A lot of the same things happen to divorcées as to widows and widowers, and a divorcée can't keep a picture of a lost partner on the bureau.

But life goes on, I forget just why, as Edna St. Vincent Millay said, and after the breakup comes the reality of money worries, suddenly cooling friendships with couples, problems with the kids, and duties you are not familiar with and that were not your job before. Some of us get bitter, and some of us feel lost, and often there's a heavy mixture of loss of self-esteem in the draft.

And some of us, emerging from the alchemy of anger, pain, and broken hopes, finally discover who we are.

One thing we learn right away, separated, widowed, or divorced, is that the world is made up of pairs. Couples tend to look to other couples for their friendships, nicely balanced twos and fours that present no tiresome problems with restaurant checks, movie tickets, and space in automobiles. Newly single women are about as socially sought after as a bad cold, and even men, popularly thought to be the hostess's dream, do not have an easy ride.

"I learned very rapidly," says George Franklin, a divorced retired navy man doing consultant work on a project in Rockville, Maryland, "that after five o'clock no one really cared what I did."

Compounding the pain and the shedding of the traces of the old life is the often acrimonious distribution of goods accumulated, the sorting out of mine and thine, and the attendant lawyers with their bills and their claims and counterclaims. And worst of all, the impossibility of explaining to troubled children that Mommy and Daddy aren't going to live together anymore, but of course they will always love them the same as before and still be their Mommy and Daddy. Only now they'll have *two* homes like Sarah in their class at school, and sure, they can bring the hamster.

Women have a hard time understanding that having a husband who wants a divorce doesn't mean that they are universally unlovable. In the rap sessions of the support organizations for new singles the self-doubts are thick in the air. Men who have been faced with a broken marriage are inclined to spot their traitorous ex-wife in all women. "I'll never trust another woman" gets squeezed out through a lot of clenched teeth.

You hear the stories over and over again in discussion sessions of Parents Without Partners: "She just took the kids and moved out while I was at work, and I was the last to find out." "We hear it both ways," sayd Dena Jansen, who handles community relations at the District of Columbia chapter. "We try to make them understand that it's okay to talk about the pain."

Everybody agrees that the death of a marriage brings regrets about the past and in their wake a disorganized present. Personal lives become radically changed, and the new life requires different skills, probably rusty skills that fell into disuse during the marriage. Many women who were once full-time wives and mothers suddenly find themselves out looking for a job in competiton with young college graduates. What's more, they've forgotten how to send out signals that men find interesting. Men discover they can't take care of themselves. They don't know which laundry does their shirts, and if they came from a traditional marriage with an unemployed wife, they may think that food magically appears on the table because they get hungry.

Linda Weatherbee, director of one of the seven area chapters of metropolitan Washington, D.C., Parents Without Partners, says that many more children are awarded to the father these days than one might think in view of the courts' natural bias toward the mother as guardian.

"Because the mother doesn't have enough money?" I ask her.

"Because she has no interest," says Weatherbee. "She wants to be independent, and children tie you down."

When Geoffrey L. Greif, a doctoral candidate at the Columbia University School of Social Work reported on what he says is the first national study of divorced and separated fathers raising children alone, he found it's more common for young women than for men to end a marriage. These women might, of course, simply be recognizing a sinking ship or cutting loose from already meaningless bonds, but nevertheless they were the instigators. It skews the picture of the brave little ex-wife clustering the children about her and weeping. Especially when Greif found it was not uncommon for the children to *choose* to live with Daddy or, for a variety of reasons, for Mommy voluntarily to give up custody.

Neighbors and friends watching a divorced father raise children alone tend to rate him as superhuman, breathing air more rarefied than do the rest of us. Greif, who has read the questionnaires, shakes his head. "These men are just average everyday Joe's," he says. Dustin Hoffman showed this guy to us in *Kramer vs. Kramer*, the harried male struggling to be both mother and father, a role in which, according to the latest guess, about six hundred thousand men are currently cast. They're not martyrs, says Greif. He's talked to some of them, and he ought to know. They *want* to do what they're doing.

What's it like being father and mother to growing kids?

Well, there's a lot of pain and confusion, but the relationship with the children is pretty rewarding.

Commander Ralph McPherson, sixty and retired, got his divorce along with three minor children after a marriage of twenty-one years.

"We'd grown apart over a period of years," says McPherson, "and when it really happened, all I felt was relief. She believed she suffered from rheumatoid arthritis and she took prescription drugs in combination with alcohol to the point where I noticed a severe personality change.

"We had financial difficulties. We lived in Texas, which is a community-property state, and when I'd close down the charge accounts, she'd come right along behind me and open them all up again. We suffered horrendous debt."

McPherson is working as a consultant and part of the pain he felt came from his inevitable isolation. He leaned on Parents Without Partners and found it useful. It helps to discover there are others with the same problems. People shore each other up.

If you have a picture in your mind of the divorced father as a stiff-upper-lip sort of guy, reading the kids to sleep and prepared to clean up the bathroom as soon as they're safely tucked in bed, you're wrong. Again and again the new feeling that it's okay to feel betrayed, hurt, and lonely crops up. Even the older divorced fathers have packed away the image of tough guys who take what is dished out. Divorced men of all ages in the eighties don't feel disgraced by tears.

"I got a phone call one morning at the office," says Harry Southbladt, a forty-year-old salesman, "asking me why I hadn't told the neighbors I was moving out." He wasn't, but his wife was, with his seven-year-old daughter and their furniture. He didn't even locate them for a week.

"I was left with an empty house, and I cried a lot," says Southbladt. "My wife got custody, and I got visiting rights. I had my daughter with me every two weeks after that, and it was clear to me that she was being used as a weapon against me. For a long time I didn't think women as a whole were worth much because they were all like her."

His wife remarried the day after the divorce became final, and now his daughter at fourteen is drifting away from him a little because of her own adolescent world is more engrossing. But he's come to grips with it all now and says it was easier losing a bit of his daughter because a good friend recognized the signs of adolescence and warned him.

"I've come to realize that I live in a world that I make. I'm trying to adjust, and I'm happier now. But I still have this fear of dating. I don't want to be rejected again."

The world finds it hard to believe, but the social life of divorced fathers is a fabric shot full of holes, almost as uncertain as that of divorced women. Support and admiration surround them, but, says Greif, "when the front door of the house is shut to all that support and attention, fathers still must struggle." Greif found most fathers dissatisfied with their social life. Think back to Dustin Hoffman's naked sleep-in guest encountering his small son in the hall, and the problems come a bit clearer. Sex and romance are hard to come by under the beady eyes of offspring, and that's to say nothing about the fact that all kinds of things have happened to women's expectations since these men were dating. They don't speak the current language, know the new gender word games. They find it hard to get used to women telephoning them, moving in aggressively when they first meet. It takes a while to get adjusted.

What probably happens is that with time "their need for

a surrogate mother goes down," says Greif. "They adjust to being single and begin dating for enjoyment rather than necessity."

Housework was not too difficult for most of the fathers Greif interviewed, but some, especially the older men, felt incompetent.

Take Tony Gallagher.

Call up Tony Gallagher and his answering machine will confuse you. Gallagher is in the insurance business, but he was once on the stage, and his answering machine is a well-known joke. You can't tell whether you'll be answered by a suave Japanese butler or an illiterate Irishman. Local talk shows love to call up Gallagher and find out who's at bat today on the machine.

Gallagher is president of Parents Without Partners International and has been divorced a long time, but he remembers keenly how it feels. He came home one night and found his wife had gone, just gone. "She had another man waiting in the wings," says Gallagher. "I found that out later. She got married the day after the divorce."

You don't feel pain or even wry cynicism when you talk to Gallagher. He's a graduate, and it's all behind him, filed away. But along the way, he says, he learned a lot about the male ego. He's another who says quite matter-of-factly that he found out it's okay to cry and to admit that a love gone sour hurts. And he didn't always know this.

"It's the male ego," he says. "We've found out we're not the lords of the land. We can admit it. And we know now it's okay to love our kids."

Now about this housework.

"It's the way I was brought up," he says. "Young boys couldn't be in the kitchen—that was sissy. But now I'm learning, and so are my contemporaries. If we can't cook or sew on a button, we can admit it. But if you're single for any reason, you don't know how to take care of yourself."

But now he's thinking about his children, and his voice goes soft, the amusement gone.

"I have a son, nineteen; he's in the air force. He's very sensitive and strong, a man. I still want to hold onto him, but he's a man. The hardest part of the parental role for the male ego is to think someone else can be a father to your child, actually doing a good job."

And what do women worry about when they divorce? A lot of the same things, but high on the list is money. Census Bureau figures report that 8.4 million women in 1981 were living with a child under twenty-one whose father was elsewhere. Just 22 percent of these mothers got the full child support due them. Past-due child support debt is more than $4 billion. Things got so bad in Maryland's Prince Georges County that the sheriff not too long ago ordered a before-dawn roundup of husbands delinquent in support payments, hauling them off in the paddy wagon to explain to the courts.

One reason for these delinquent payments, if we are to believe University of Pennsylvania sociologist Frank Furstenberg, Jr., and Johns Hopkins sociologist Andrew Cherlin, is that three out of four divorced fathers remarry within a few years and lose interest in the first crop of children, not to mention finding bills stemming from their new family onerous. Furstenberg, in the 1981 national study done with James Peterson and Nicholas Zill, found that half of all teenage children of divorced parents hadn't seen their fathers in the past year, a third in the past five years. Only 2 percent of the mothers in the survey claimed the fathers took too *much* interest in the children.

There's no getting around the fact that divorces grow out of ill feeling, and arrangements arising from them are not always civilized. Selma Nagy, a New York City psychologist, remembers a woman whose husband departed her life leaving her the house in Scarsdale and $100 a week to support their two children.

If you're wondering how a man who owned a house in Scarsdale could fork over such a minuscule support for his children, he had, it developed, some assets cleverly hidden away from the bulk of his money so that he looked to be less affluent than he was. The ex-wife tried her best to stretch the money.

But eventually she hired a private detective, who tracked her ex-husband to a Fifth Avenue studio apartment with his new love. In a rage the discarded wife picked up the children, one under each arm, and appeared unannounced at her husband's door. "Here," she shouted when he answered the door, "if you think you can raise them on a hundred dollars a week, do it yourself."

After that, things rearranged themselves more comfortably.

There are no absolutes, no rules in the shipwreck of a marriage, and angry groups united to push common claims spring up like mushrooms. Free Men, a liberation group in Washington, D.C., agrees that more strict laws on child support are needed but demands better visitation rights enforcement. Feminist expectations limit their role options, they claim. Fathers' rights groups have sprung up in many cities, but they're still in the minority compared to women's.

Especially in the military and foreign service, pension rights are a big stake when the divorce happens before the checks have started coming. EXPOSE, an acronym for Ex-Partners of Servicemen for Equality is a national advocacy group for divorced military ex-wives and widows. Nancy Abell, fifty-year-old legislative aid for EXPOSE has a strong feeling that the disillusion of Vietnam has dramatically changed these men and may account for their divorce rate.

"I've talked to literally hundreds of women, and I'm convinced that war changed their husbands. They weren't heroes. The American public didn't treat them very well. It wasn't even a declared war."

Nancy Abell knows something about this firsthand. Her divorced husband was a colonel in Nam. She won't talk about how it was when he came home.

Divorce in the services, Abell points out, is a real no-no,

the end of promotions. But the brake on a man's military career is nothing to what it does to the divorced wives. "I have a hard time convincing those wives that it happens often," she says. "Their self-esteem hits rock bottom."

Abell, who knows the territory, has thrown herself into trying to make things easier for these women. Until a year ago it wasn't even legal for a divorced military wife to keep medical benefits and canteen shopping rights. "My ex wanted to give me survivor benefits, and he couldn't. We got that changed," says Abell. "Now the states decide if a man can designate an ex-spouse as beneficiary, but it must be a voluntary decision. No court can order it. If he doesn't make a decision in a year, the new wife gets it."

What Nancy Abell says is true. The Vietnam experience did change, maybe forever, a lot of military husbands. Dr. Raymong M. Scurfield, assistant director for readjustment counseling for the Veterans Administration, felt the problem was so important that he asked the Congress to appropriate money for a survey on how the needs of these men could best be met.

"The veterans were very young," says Dr. Scurfield, "and their first year or two back was particularly problematical. Part of the issues had to do with the trauma they had witnessed. A number were involved in killings of women and children, and it had a heavy influence on their own intimate relations. They'd lost close friends and found it difficult to make new ones. And difficult to trust again.

"They had tremendous difficulty talking about all of this. They felt people weren't interested or else very judgmental. Some had arms and legs gone, and they got the impression they had had lost parts of their body uselessly. They had a lot of anger against the army and the government, and a lot of this got directed at wives.

"It got bottled up inside them.

"Added to this was that they went over alone and came back alone. They were assigned to units over there, and they came back individually when their tour was over, melting back into their lives without really dealing with what had happened."

Dr. Scurfield thinks a moment.

"And the funny thing is," he says, "there are people from World War II who had the same trouble. I've had people come up to me after I spoke in Rotary, maybe, who tell me that's just the way it is with their husbands. There was this wall there, and they couldn't penetrate the wall."

Elizabeth Jane Myers is a sweet-faced woman of sixty-two, who for thirty-five years was married to a navy captain who divorced her for another woman to whom he was married just thirty-nine days before he died. For thirty-five years Elizabeth Jane followed him from post to post with no thought of building a career of her own. Today his pension payments go to the wife of his short-lived marriage, and Elizabeth Myers has gone to work in a department store in Chesapeake, Virginia, to support herself.

Elizabeth Myers didn't want to talk about it when I first dialed her number in Virginia Beach where she lives.

"I've had some strange calls since that article came out in the newspaper with my picture and the story."

I can imagine. One of the threads of the story was that her friends had awarded her the honorary title of "Thrown Away Military Wife of the Month."

It said nothing in the story about where her husband had been stationed just before the breakup, but I took a guess.

"Was he by any chance in Vietnam?" I asked her.

He was. When he came back, he didn't talk about it. It was as if there was this wall. Then came the divorce.

Since then Myers has had four jobs, not counting a year off to take care of her grandchildren. She works now with a good group of people, she says, but she doesn't discuss her difficulty with them. But her friend, Doris Mosley, has gotten her into a group she formed called the Committee for Justice and Equality for the Military Wife, which hopes to get for dumped wives the same pro rata pension rights that spouses of Foreign Service and CIA wifes have enjoyed since 1981. Pensions for these women are prorated on the basis of length of marriage unless a divorce court intervenes.

"It's the navy makes it hard," says Myers in her gentle voice. "The system needs to be changed."

Doris Mosley's group helped in other ways. It put her in touch with other people like her. "There are a lot of us out there," says Myers.

I had never met the woman before but I liked her immediately. She was beautifully dressed and her accent was European. Her eyes said she'd seen a lot of things she'd have preferred not to, but she had learned a good deal along the way.

In the musical chairs of the post-dinner hour she dropped down beside me on the sofa, and somehow it came out very early that her son was in the process of getting divorced.

I smiled with what I thought was sympathy, but she laid a cool hand on my arm and frowned.

"You smile," she said. "Do not smile. It is a tragedy. Great tragedy."

She gave me the story then, unfolding it like a Greek myth, and if I had wondered how she could care so much when it was once removed from her and hardly unusual at that, I saw that I had displayed lack of imagination.

"My son is devastated," she said over the rim of her cordial glass. "I also suffer. He is a difficult man sometimes, like my own husband, but he always loved her. Once when he was fifteen, he sought out and knocked down another young man who was taken with her. He grew up and married her, and he loves her still. She wants a divorce."

"Another man?" I murmur. "A coup de foudre?"

"She says not. She is so beautiful, so talented, a lawyer.

He rose and she rose, and they are both so successful, and they were so happy. She came to tell me, and she said she hoped it would not interfere with our friendship."

I asked her what she replied.

"I cast my eyes down," she said, casting them down now to show me. It had a devastating effect.

"Three children," she said.

"If there is no other man, why did she do it?"

"She says, 'I have to think of me.' "

I never met the young woman or her ex-husband who loves her still, but she haunts me in odd moments. Such ripples of pain spread out from her decision, and her words seem to evoke the whole world of self-fulfillment so fashionable today, though it might well have no deeper meaning than that her husband and she turned ultimately to be different breeds of cats.

Finally, I called Dr. Baxter who, in his work at the Marriage and Family Institute in Washington, sees this kind of thing every day.

Is it possible, I asked him, that in some cases divorce has a very positive effect for at least one member of the former couple?

He suggested that it was indeed possible that some individuals are very surprised to find out much of their potential is realized after divorce. "But not without work," he warned. "Not without a network of support. Therapy and support groups that help you to learn to accept pain, to stop saying there must have been something I should have done."

Support groups. Alcoholics Anonymous must have been the granddaddy of them all, and its lineal descendants are legion. Built on the old truth that misery loves company and it helps to know someone else who also knows the territory, they've come into their own in the age of group therapy. Nearly everyone agrees that they help.

Carol Randolph of Takoma Park, Maryland, knows something about this. After a two-year marriage she was separated and found she didn't know many people who were separated.

So she put an ad in the *Washingtonian* magazine asking people who had the same problem to call. That's how New Beginnings, a Takoma Park support group for men and women suffering the dislocation of early separation and divorce, began. The group now has close to four hundred members, men and women ranging from their twenties to the senior member of seventy years.

Randolph finds it especially trying that people assume that if you're young and divorced you have no problem.

" 'You're young, you'll find somebody else,' they say. This discounts all the pain the person is feeling, especially if that person doesn't have children, as if *because* he or she is young and doesn't have children it should be a snap to get on with life. In fact, for someone like myself, at thirty-two, divorce may mean they will *never* have children. I am too aware of how bad a bad marriage can be, so I don't want to marry just to have kids. But if I don't remarry rather soon, I may *also* have to give up the dream of motherhood."

Randolph, divorced and anxious to explore how others feel, has quit her job as an executive assistant in a trade association in order to nurture New Beginnings full-time. As executive director she now has a salary paid from membership fees, which are a hefty $25 per person. She feels good about the work she does.

"Separation is a nowhere place," she says. "People don't talk about it. I don't fit in with my neighbors. I think belonging is important." She thinks she's making it possible for singles to belong somewhere.

Randolph says that when she was married she was a "clutchy, clingy wife." You wouldn't believe that if you met her now. When the car breaks down, the answering device goes on the fritz, it's up to her now, and it shows. The heartbeat of New Beginnings depends on her, and she copes nicely. She marshals the support for the people going through what she went through, organizes discussions, engages speakers, schedules social events, even helps members with legal difficulties. She feels the group offers an extra dimension beyond therapy, which she considers essential.

"In no way do we replace therapy. We augment it, we look at the issues, everyday issues like how to be around the members of the opposite sex. You think that's crazy?"

Randolph obviously doesn't. You get out of practice during a marriage.

She has no children, and at New Beginnings the assumption naturally is that you do. She hasn't remarried, but like the rest would be happy to find the right person. "There's nobody who doesn't want to be married," she says, and her tone does not allow for doubt.

I asked her if she thought more compromises were involved in second marriages.

"I was a second wife," she says. "A rebound. I'd like to have someone to share the good stuff with. But I think you have to give yourself a year to find out who you are. If you give yourself that much time, you can make realistic decisions. It's probably going to be a more mature love. I don't think coup de foudre is love. Anything but."

In that year and through the pain of loss what you have to learn is communication skills, she says. "Learn to fight."

Once she asked the senior member of New Beginnings what could possibly happen to a marriage of over forty years to cause the breakup.

"I didn't want the next ten years to be like the last ten," he said cheerfully.

Randolph's ex-husband hasn't remarried either.

"He moved in with his mother," says the ex-clutchy, clinging wife, grinning.

Divorcées, male or female, cope with various degrees of success with their new singleness, according to their temperament, but one skill that comes in especially handy in picking up the pieces is feeling comfortable about being alone. Being single involves a lot of time alone unless you rush around frenetically to keep from being left with only yourself. Widows know this and so do divorcees. And eventually what you had to learn to do becomes a need. I can attest to this. After seven years alone I have come to the point where I can't be with someone every hour of the day, no matter how charming. I need solitude in regular doses, and the last time I had a houseguest I finally had to excuse myself for a moment or two alone with myself. "To think about the international situation," I told him as he gazed at me, puzzled but polite.

The English have always understood this. They provide maps of the countryside for their houseguests and go off about their own business, calling back cheerily that everyone will meet for tea. Reading a book for an hour or two is looked on favorably, solitary moments respected.

"If you can't be alone, it's an affliction," Caroline Nelson, a divorcee of ten years, said to me. "I love being alone."

We're sitting in her pretty living room, me on the sofa in my golf skirt with the cat in my lap and she across from me wearing something soft and pink, from Saks probably, because she works there in the better dress department. The cat, she tells me, is her daughter's, a summer boarder now on the dope cure after having had his Meow Mix laced with marijuana in a fraternity house at her daughter's college.

"He's so much better," says Caroline comfortably. "He was kind of crazy till I got him cold turkey. Name's Chicken Little."

"Were you born liking to have time to yourself?" I inquire over Chicken Little's head. "Or did you learn it after your divorce? Did you love him when you married him?"

"What is love?" she says in the soft accents of the South so that it somehow sounds very profound. "I was twenty-five and I thought it was time to marry. That's what people did. He was very attractive. His three children from his first marriage would live with their mother.

"I waited on him," she says over the rim of her glass. "He'd say, 'Get me a glass of water. Change this bed.' I was brought up in that era. I think it's marvelous how the young women handle it all today."

It took her husband about a year to rearrange things so that his children came to him and Caroline. Little by little he became a semi-invalid, combining liquor with Quaaludes, Librium, and Valium. They drifted apart.

"We didn't go to parties together; we sat in different rooms at home. On my fortieth birthday I told him I'd like to be free, but it was ten years later, when he had another woman waiting in the wings, that we got a divorce.

"When I told my mother about the divorce arrangements, she said, 'What are you doing, trying to get money from him? When it's over, a lady bows out.' I never spoke to her again."

Chicken Little purrs and rubs his whiskers on my arm. In the kitchen the phone rings, and I wait till Caroline speaks briefly with her daughter.

"Did you think of marrying again?" I ask her when she reappears. Caroline is easy and friendly with people. She's been divorced ten years, and in that time there must have been some kind of flick.

"I located the man once, but my daughter said, 'Oh, wonderful, he's just like Daddy.' "

She didn't do it. And doesn't think much about it now.

On the floor is a huge pile of library books, and she watches me trying to read the titles upside down.

"I love reading," she says. "After I work all day, it's so nice to come home to this house and the quiet. All day at Saks I talk to people."

I told her what Shirley McLaine said to a reporter interviewing her for the *Ladies Home Journal*: "I don't need a man to ratify my existence. The most profound relationship we'll ever have is with ourselves."

She thinks this over silently, and I inquire if her husband remarried.

Her smile is bemused.

"He died two weeks after the divorce."

Caroline looks comfortable with herself. Totally at ease, a graduate doing very nicely, thank you, having learned a lot since she was twenty-five. "Of course," she says, "I am appalled at the divorce thing now, six months after the altar. But then there's no question of alimony. You just divide up the bills."

My cousin, whom we all called Toodie Lambo, was married five times and divorced the first time when she was pregnant with her first child. She was very pretty, a round, blonde, blue-eyed prettiness that made things easy for her, but nothing worked out for very long. She was the only child of my aunt Mary, who was pleased with the idea of a daughter but never seemed quite to know what to do with her. She called her "my little toodie-lambo" and paid the older cousins ten cents an hour to play with her while she pursued a life that included too many cocktails.

Toodie was my friend, which isn't always true of cousins. I was in her first wedding when she got married at seventeen, and I saw a lot of her until that marriage went sour and she put her apartment up for sublet. She married a man who answered her sublet ad, and he drove her to Reno to get her divorce, trying to stay in major cities en route in case the baby was born. They got married in Reno. I liked that husband, but I lost track after that.

She's dead now, having died very young, so I can't ask her anything about picking up the pieces after a divorce, which she seemed to do so promptly. I never even met the last two husbands, and I have no idea what she was thinking, this pretty, vulnerable young woman who started out with so much. Around the pool, in the jukebox joints of the time, in the twin beds of the guest room of another aunt we talked about love, but we never talked about failure. I have a strong feeling that my cousin Toddie Lambo never grew up and found out who she was. She had a picture of herself as a wife, and she kept trying different leading men to see if any of them would wear. So many mistakes must have a common thread. I think the divorces weren't mistakes; the marriages were. She married for the wrong reasons.

All of this happened before women who didn't have to work worked. You graduated from college and you got married and had babies. You were slated to be somebody's wife and you knew it. It was tunnel vision. It accounts for a lot.

My pretty blonde Danish hairdresser Tova is combing me out when I ask her about her divorce, and the hairbrush never falters. It has all been dealt with, and any trouble obviously is behind her. Her face in the mirror behind me is piquant, intelligent, and engrossed. I wonder why she hasn't married again, and finally I ask her.

"After a while you're not looking anymore," she says in her soft accents, which wrap strange charming additions around *r*'s and *v*'s. "I fell in love once, but the church wouldn't forgive my divorce. I wouldn't see him anymore, and he married someone else. Now I have my work. I think if I'd had my work before it would have been all right. I think being a hausfrau is okay; it's just not my hobby."

There we are, the voice of the eighties, and you don't have to have been born in the fifties to speak with that same voice. Work gives identity, holds you together. If my cousin Toodie had had some work, things might have gone better for her.

It's funny about having been married and no longer being married. It's full of pain, but it also brings with it the ability to double-speak. You remember how it was, but you also know how it is now, which people still married do not, so that it gives you a peculiar kind of double vision they cannot share. It has a tendency to make you tot up the sum of things, and above all it binds you to other people who have had the same experience. It's like meeting a fellow countryman while traveling abroad.

This, maybe, is why Eleanor Davis and I have reforged an interrupted friendship based on a college acquaintance of forty years ago. Both of us have learned things along the way that we didn't know last time we met, and the things that have happened to us have changed us into more the same kind of person.

Eleanor is back in the small New England island where she spent her childhood summers, and it's the first time since her divorce. She says, on her handsome blue-green stationery that reminds me of the color the Maine ocean is not, that this little house she kept throughout her marriage is the one constant in her life. It goes way back to the days when Sid and Joe Adams put snakes in bottles on her doorstep because they knew she was afraid of snakes. The third and seventh steps still creak as they did when she avoided them so as not to wake her parents en route to bed after some torrid lovemaking on the living room floor below in front of the fire. Her children's growing height is marked in pencil on the newell post, and the girl she was and the woman she became is everywhere in this little house.

The memories get mixed up together into some sort of a lifetime, and she can still see her father's memorial service in the little graveyard up the road where Mr. Gerrard, postmaster cum minister, spilled her father's ashes in the gutter on the way to the cemetery and had to get down on his knees to scoop them up. She remembers her mother looking little and frail and alone waving good-bye, and the image gets mixed up with her own.

It was here that she received an expected check from her ex-husband who had forgotten to put the zip code on the envelope. It had wandered around for two weeks before it reached her, with a penciled notation: NOT AT THE SCHOOL FOR THE DEAF.

"I long to write to him," wrote Eleanor, "that aging as I am, I am most certainly *not* at the Governor Baxter School for the Deaf, but alive and well and living at zip code 04003. Somehow I suppose this is the sort of thing you can't share with a former mate without sounding petulant. In divorce the jokes are totally different. That would be the kind of intimacy no longer allowed."

Divorce is a nowhere place.

Chapter

9

*The Second Time
Around*

Why do you want to get married again, friends at the Philadelphia Inquirer asked Art Carey. The question was heavy with implications. When you're doing so well on the singles circuit, why go out of your way to sign another contract?

Carey is a thirty-four-year-old, old-line Philadelphia, Princeton graduate, and he speaks in the venacular, embellished slightly with phrases lifted from F. Scott Fitzgerald. "Sports fucking isn't enough," he said. "You need someone to hang onto in the real dark night of the soul."

I took that same question to my friend Lucy, who was a twenty-five-year-old widow with two kids at the time she remarried the first time.

"I wanted a normal life for my children," she said, "and I was a sitting duck. They all wanted to climb in bed with me."

This last, of course, was in the 1940s and might, therefore, be in another country, but it's one reason still. And in between lies every variation, every shade of human need that drives us, male and female, four times out of five, to have another go with the marriage vows. The Census Bureau keeps its neat records without much comment, but it does point out that increasing age in women works directly against remarriage and that divorcées, whether male or female, are much more likely to remarry than widows and widowers. This may have something to do with the relative age of each, but if love's more comfortable the second time around, you can't prove it by older women.

Still and all, if you're a man or a woman under forty, you'll probably be back to try again. And according to who we are and what we learned the first time around, we apparently bring different strengths and expectations to the new marriage.

Art Carey, self-described one-time jock, arrived at his second marriage after almost classic progression through the three stages of postdivorce readjustment described by Dr. Isiah Zimmerman, a McLean, Virginia, psychologist. Neatly outlined, these stages look like a patient's fever chart, and clearly not everyone will follow the course. But in uncharted seas of disillusionment and disappointment, not to say pain and self-doubt, it's nice to consider the path others tread. Dr. Zimmerman sees the stages as figuring out your old mistakes, becoming aware that the possibility of a new commitment is warring with fear of being hurt again, and final emergence into a whole new chance for happiness.

Or as Art Carey puts it, maturing little by little, in stages.

"I was right out of Princeton, and I thought the major problem of marriage would be walking down the aisle. I had no idea that marriage would require constant cultivation. We had separate interests, and while she was spending her time with the horsey set, I got to spending my time with male friends. I was jocking out."

He met his present wife, Tanya, at a suburban volleyball game in Bucks County.

"The city editor of the labor journal I was working on

introduced us," says Carey. "She'd come east because her marriage was coming apart. She had a job in clinical research at the University of Pennsylvania. I was still married.

"I heard later she asked who the macho hot dog was."

When Carey got divorced, his editor/friend gave him Tanya's phone number, and from the first date they hit it off.

Why wasn't she just another notch in a long progression of conquests?

"She played her cards right," says Carey, and it's clear he doesn't see this as macho. "She played the role of experienced woman because she'd been divorced longer. She told me to go out and have my fling; she'd be there when I got through."

He had his fling. He makes no bones that sexual performance is important to him. Missing from his first marriage was what he calls passion, and now he was making up for it. He had been physically attracted to his first wife, but "there were no fireworks in the sack." It got worse: "We were roommates." Freed of the marriage he dated several Playmates, found the sexual chase almost too easy.

It was all great fun, but eventually he found it unsatisfyingly ephemeral and began to reassess. "You can't hold five women when you're feeling terrified."

He began to think about marrying again, but he was beset by doubts. "I went through great ambivalence," he says now with the air of a combat veteran who has survived the worst. "Once burned, twice shy. Every night I tossed and turned, thinking about the pros and cons of marriage, and one night I got up and listed them all in a balance sheet on a yellow legal pad. They were pretty commonplace, but the thing that most appealed to me was that it gave you a place to come to. Still, I was terrified of commitment, and we broke up for four months."

Finally, he asked Tanya to marry him and everything fell into place. They've been married now for two years and are about to become parents. And what has he got in his second marriage that he didn't have before?

"More maturity."

Clearly your passport in the single life is a different color if you're a woman and especially a woman with a child.

"Tell me how you felt when you decided to marry again," I said to Lucy. I didn't know her then, though we came from the same part of upstate New York.

"I thought you'd never ask," she says, settling back on her rose-colored sofa and kicking off well-polished loafers to examine an incipient blister. The word for Lucy is forthright, and you know it right away when you meet her. It's written in the way she sits, one hand draped over the back of the chair, the tone of her voice, the dearth of minced words, the tilt of her chin. You know where you are with Lucy.

"I told you," she says, straightening up and trying to collect from her brain files how it felt to be twenty-five. "Everybody wanted to hop in bed with me."

"All right, Jezebel, are you trying to tell me you married to escape being sexually pursued?"

She thinks about this, excusing the blister from scrutiny. She's been married three times and it takes thought.

"I married to give my children a normal home life."

"You mean you married to have a father for the kids?" Financial security has never been her problem. She was born with it.

"That's about it."

"What happened to love?"

Her silence is eloquent. The marriage was a disaster. She's thumbing through those mind files again. "You know, it's funny," she says after a while. "Maybe I knew from the start it wasn't going to work. I never took my ten-year-old out of boarding school. Why don't you stay for dinner?"

"It wasn't that I needed companionship," continues Lucy after we have put away a plate of lightly browned sweetbreads and a salad. She leans back in her chair and studies the topmost branches of her four-hundred-year-old oak tree under which we are having coffee. "I wanted a normal home life. I bought the house we lived in, and then he was called to Washington, and he rented a house for us that wasn't big enough. My daughter was sleeping in the dining room, and we had another boy by then. We needed a bigger house, and I told him to find one and I'd live in it. But it didn't work out that way. So I bought a Washington house. This house. He didn't even decide to come with us until the movers arrived."

It's a nice house, Lucy's house. It has the furniture she inherited and a splendid grand piano and a handsome garden with the oak tree. And pictures of the three children for whom, or for two of whom, she went looking for a normal life. Portraits and photographs of them and their children on the table, the piano, the bookcase.

We argue often about those pictures.

"There's no class to a mess of family photographs," I tell her. "Worn orientals speak of old money, important status, and there you're doing fine. Very classy holes in the rug to trip people. We have to take away points for photos on the piano."

She smiles. Her children dominate her life. She likes it that way.

"I'm telling you the rest," she says. "Let me finish. He got an offer of a position in Denver and he took it. It was clear he didn't care whether I went or not. I didn't go. He went alone."

So in the end it didn't turn out to be a normal life for the children either.

"Why do you think most women marry again?" I ask Lucy, who is pouring us more coffee.

"They marry," says Lucy, who knows no more than anyone else but when asked for an opinion gives one, "for financial support."

Money, of course, cuts both ways. Ask Fatima, my wonderful longtime friend and cleaning woman who lives with her daughter and her granddaughter and grandson in what I imagine to be a multigenerational Eden of understanding. Her daughter, I think, could buy and sell me several times, judging from the nippy little car in which she picks up her mother. Her granddaughter is doing well in home care, but it's her grandson who deeply fascinates me. That's because Fatima told me that sometimes when she's just sitting there watching television he gets up and strides across the room just to hug her. Sometimes he knocks her glasses askew, says Fatima.

I never met anyone who did that, and I am impressed.

For this dynasty and a parallel one from a son living close by, Fatima, left a widow, married a second time. "I had all those children," she told me once, "and my husband was dead."

Fatima keeps her own counsel. Alongside her, Calvin Coolidge would have been considered garrulous. But in the course of twenty-eight years together—one day a week—I have pieced together her life.

"Did your children like their stepfather?"

Me, prying.

"Well," she says, staying her mop in her reluctance to say anything bad about anyone. "They like him all right."

I don't get it all in any day, not even in any one month. Troubles, I understand, are not to be complained about, though we courteously inquire of each other about bad knees.

"I guess the money helped," I venture. Money clearly makes trouble coming and going, too much or too little.

"It helped."

"Was it a good marriage?" I finally blurt out.

"Not like the first," she says, on her knees, folding trash bags for storage under the sink. "I wasn't used to all that drinkin'."

Even friends can go just so far. Maybe somehow it was

worthwhile. Such a nice warm, loving family of children. And they liked him all right.

"Financial security is not as strong a factor today as it used to be," says Dr. Shirley Zussman, a New York Psychologist whose doctorate is in family studies and education. "In the second marriage even older women have arrived at some way of meeting the bills—inheritance or salary, something."

Money does undeniably weight the scales. Even men these days don't especially like to feel it's all up to them, says Dr. Zussman. Hardly ever do you hear them murmur, "Let me take care of you, little girl." Money makes a difference.

Practical considerations sneak into the act the second time around—whether your dogs would get along, whose house you will choose to live in, is this guy a good father for your kids or just a lover?

Love and marriage get increasingly complicated with possessions that accumulated the first time around. Judy Wheatland, divorcing her husband, Rex, turned down $20,000 for her share of Runaway, half cocker, half poodle, though her bank account at the time showed $15, according to newspaper reports. A woman recently hit the headlines when she allegedly shot the children of her previous marriage because they were in the way of a second marriage. Premarital agreements are making lawyers rich.

The husband of a friend of mine asked, when they split, for the electric frying pan. He didn't see how he could cook without the electric frying pan. Apparently a new one would not have been the same. My friend refused.

But of all the complications that make a second marriage less simple than the first, stepchildren are way out in front. Donna Coffey, a family therapist in Valencia, California, finds one special situation again and again in her work: the stepfather asked to discipline children from the first marriage.

"The new wife expects her husband to give her children

the discipline she thinks they need, but the kids rebel. They complain when he moves in to try it, and she turns around and takes their side. It's a double bind."

Not quite so common but cropping up with some frequency is the natural father who has custody of the children and remarries. Things in his household have been kind of loose, and the second wife wants to inject a little order into the house once it's hers. Or she wants a new house and a fresh start with a shipshape crew. It makes for rebellion.

Young second wives can get flack from an adolescent daughter still with the father. With the male tendency to marry a younger woman, she may be only a decade or so older than the stepdaughter she is bringing up. The replacement for her own mother sometimes makes the stepdaughter antagonistic, and that's putting it charitably.

Possessions complicate, but basic among the drives pushing us toward a second try at the altar is the immutable rule of the culture: couples can deal more easily with the world as it is. Maybe it takes two to survive. Well.

"We're a married society," says Dr. Zussman. "Being on your own may have some advantages, but ties are more pleasant. Alone is more fragmented. Generally we want companionship."

We both consider companionship briefly as a compelling reason for marriage. I allow myself indulgently to imagine what it would be like to say "we" again—*we* think, *we* like them so much, *we* never have broccoli— when Dr. Zussman interrupts my fantasy with an example of ESP that must be quite an asset in her labors in muddled lives.

"You know what really intrigues me?" she inquires, and her voice comes alive with interest.

What really intrigues Dr. Zussman is the—no, wait, let me put it this way—dining room tables.

Dining room tables?

"When I was growing up, mealtimes were taken for granted. We expected to sit down to a meal around the table, sitting down, all of us, at the end of the day. And now in my clinical practice I've discovered there's no such thing anymore. You've got two people coming home—six, seven, eight o'clock—and nobody expects to make a real meal. They're going off to karate class or aerobics, and the kids get fed quickly. Where I live, every other store is a take-out food place. And I bet it is where you live too.

"The men pay lip service to equal rights (to shared cooking chores), but it's hard to forgo what they remember in the past. You can't expect it now."

I don't expect she was saying that an evening meal and a pause in the day's occupations could knit up a marital rift but was only reporting her observations on expectations. But I was busy running pictures of my own dining room table, once my mother's, a Victorian table with griffin legs, claw-footed and toenailed, around which my family gathered for years. All through the sixties the rules of that table remained steadfastly constant, and by Booth's order, no male sat at it without tie and jacket, while females honored it with a skirt. Below table we might be barefooted, but this ritual meal, even if it was only tuna fish casserole, was a formal moment with lighted candles. Around that table the disasters of every day were muted, avoided, or glossed over. Around that table we were a family unit, mutually supportive, if at no other time. You were promoted to that table when you were old enough, and it was an honor. When we brought Joan home from the hospital, her brother looked at her, swathed in the nursery blanket, and remarked, "Now I'll never have to eat alone again."

If Dr. Zussman is right, dining room tables along with dining rooms have become an endangered species, having disappeared along with expectations of the evening meal. I regret that. I suppose you could say we communicated around that table, though we thought we were just eating.

And unless I miss my guess, when Art Carey says you need someone to hold onto and Lucy says she wanted a normal life for her children, dining room tables and what happens around them have something to do with what they're talking about. A place to come back to.

Even twenty-eight-year-old Lisa Wolfson, the investment wonder who earns or did earn more than $100,000 annually in a brokerage firm and has one failed marriage behind her, told *Esquire*, which spotlighted her as a prime example of the New Woman, that what she was most afraid of was loneliness. I thought I'd call her up and ask her more about that, but she had quit her job and the trail grew cold, though I left a network of messages. It seemed to me that she mentioned to *Esquire* that her dreams for the future included a bookshop and a couple of kids, but it was the loneliness that caught my imagination. Because it's just easier to fit in when you're one of a pair, a team against a world that doesn't care.

Yes, but do we learn anything the first time? Surely one of the things we find out from a lousy marriage is that there are worse things than being alone. But probably we find that out gradually, some more quickly than others. Liz Carpenter thinks so.

"The first year after divorce or death you're looking," she says. "I've got a friend who told me the first year she'd have married Sammy Davis, Jr. After that you're not on the hunt for anything permanent—unless it's red hot. Leave that clause. The main thing is to feel that you're needed and you can find the other ways.

"I asked Clare Boothe Luce once if 'the women' were still 'the women,' the very wealthy, and she said they're still tuned to the same things as when she wrote about them, but they don't want to remarry. They love to go to the hairdresser and get all fixed up and go out with the boys, but by the time they've got the money straightened out they don't want to mess it up with another marriage."

There are no statistics to prove it, but the evidence seems to point to the inescapable fact that blind, all-consuming love is less often involved the second time around. Caution tossed for the second time to the winds happens but not with any regularity.

Men, so wary of making the commitment the first time, seem to look for a replacement more quickly as they age. In their palmier days, they move more slowly, both the first and second time. Freedom becomes less precious as the hair begins to gray, whereas women seem to rely on their female support network in lieu of marriage. There are, of course, many women who simply can't live alone, and unspoken bargains arise out of this: I'll see that your home is well managed, you see that the car gets tuned and headwaiters don't snub me; or, I'll bring amusing people into your life, and you figure out how the bank thinks my mortgage bonds are a mistake.

The wrenching noise of expectations being lowered is deafening.

"What were you looking for the second time around?" I asked a man who, as a widower, embarked on a new marriage that lasted five months.

"Someone just like my first wife."

"Did you love her?" I inquire sternly. "The second one?" One of these days I'm going to be told to bug off.

"I liked her."

Widowed people, both men and women, are slower to remarry in the early years than divorced people, a fact no expert undertook to explain to me. Given the imbalance between the marriageable men and women, it's probable that any man who is not a falling-down drunk or on welfare can marry at his pleasure, and it's odd to discover well-heeled, attractive men playing the bachelor game forever after their wives die. I asked an old friend of mine, who spends his vacation traveling with single women of his acquaintance, why he never married after his first wife, Helen, died of cancer.

He didn't sound changed in the four years since we last met. The same warm voice, the same cordial glad surprise to hear from an old friend again. Gerry is a pleasant fellow.

We caught each other up on the years since last we talked and then I asked him why he, a catch really, had not wanted to try again.

"Maybe I was just too happy the first time," he tells me, laughing to show he knows it's all out of style, the mourner at the grave, straight out of those Victorian prints with a weeping willow and a child in high-button shoes off to one side. In the background I can hear Liza Minelli belting it out on his stereo, remembering that it was a good time, it was the best time, and we thought that it would last forever. "It's a hard act to follow."

I know something about that, I tell him.

"And I've got three wonderful kids," he goes on, "and I wonder if I remarried, if it would make a difference. And I've been lucky in the women I know who keep me from being lonesome."

There's a pause.

"But of course two of them got married recently."

How does he manage the house?

"I've been very lucky," he says again, and I can see he is really happy. "A dynamite housekeeper." As happy as he expects to be.

Work holds people together, not to mention paying the gas bill. It keeps their edges honed. The need to work might even be a backhanded gift of the gods to make up for their other lousy deals. Money insulates people. People who work have a reason to get up in the morning beyond wondering how they'll kill the day. It's even possible that a bad marriage or widowhood might be a chance to find out who you are.

"Did you know you weren't a hausfrau before you married." I asked Tova, my hairdresser, once when she was cutting my hair, "or after you went to work?"

She only laughed and I got to thinking, when she had put away the scissors, of all the women I knew who once were married and now live alone, supporting themselves. Which made me think of Eileen, an editor of mine in New York with whom, by WATS line, courtesy of her office, I often exchange opinions on marriage, men, the stock market, dogs, daughters, and automobile insurance. I have no idea how old she is, since neither of us would dream of asking such a question. No good could possibly come of it. I do know she has been a widow for some time and that there are men in her life, none of whom she will probably marry. She's been working out her life ever since I've known her, and when she told me she'd met a new man, I asked if anything in her thinking had changed.

"I guess," she says in a lilting accent straight out of Dublin where she was born, "that I've arrived at the point in my life when I'm content to live alone."

Pause.

"But perhaps I don't know it yet. I'm not content to compromise."

Art Carey chronicled his trip through the sexual pleasures of the single world by drawing up the pluses and minuses of remarriage. He is lyrically happy with Tanya, and Gerry is reasonably happy with his traveling women and his housekeeper, Tova with her hairdressing. And as I keep forgetting, my own marriage was a second try for Booth, who once stood by a hotel bureau in Syracuse, New York, wearing very little else besides his army hat, and caught my wrist to whisper fiercely, "If this doesn't work out, I'll never believe in anything again."

I can't remember that we needed good reasons to marry, and it did work out. All of which only goes to prove that there are no rules but the ones we make up as we go along.

Joan, being part of the new wave, might, I thought, have some light to shed. I broached the subject when she next dropped by for a cup of tea.

"I think," I began, stirring my tea meditatively, "that the only reason for marriage the first or second or fifth time is because anything else is unthinkable. Over to you."

I gave her some time to think it over, since she was speaking for a generation with a divorce record that has surpassed all records up to now.

It came out nicely phrased.

"One reason for the high divorce rate is not that we feel dissatisfied that ours is not the perfect mate but we marry for the wrong reasons. I mean because we're the right age or we're tired of going to singles bars or we just got divorced.

"And it's just more fun than being alone."

10

*The Devaluation
of the
Middle-aged Woman:
What Lies Ahead
at Thirty*

One of my close friends lived and died without telling me her age. Of the rest, I know the age of about half. In America today a woman's age is a closely guarded trade secret. If it's over thirty, public knowledge of it works to her disadvantage socially, economically, and in nearly every close encounter.

Not so with men. It is perfectly permissible for men to age. On them a few lines and gray hair at the temples speak of experience, power, and savoir faire. On women they announce "over the hill." Heaven forbid that she should be thought to have experience. Experience in a woman is a dirty word. The women's movement had better take this up next, and some job it will be. America is youth oriented. The hair dye people and the plastic surgeons have grown rich helping women to appear young. Next best to being young, of course, is to look young.

A cleaning lady I once had told me this is not so in Korea, where she was born. "Natural Mother write lines on face and nobody cares. They just go on living," she says, briskly flicking her dust mop. "Mostly I love this country, but not that." Her hand on the mop handle is angry, and I step out of range of her furniture polish spray can.

In Europe, the movies tell us, mature women can still find love. Maybe not a new husband, but love. Here, when Shirley MacLaine let her dye job grow out to show the roots in the final scenes of *Terms of Endearment*, Hollywood breathed respectful gasps of admiration for what an actress would suffer for her art. In America youth is everything. The movies reflect the taste of the baby boom moviegoing customers, now in their mid-thirties, who most especially do not care for the idea of aging and would take their dollars elsewhere if much of it was reflected on the silver screen.

"Don't make me smile. I might split something," says the voice of my friend Dorothy on the phone. "I think you should come over and take a picture of me for posterity to record what happens to a woman who has a facelift."

I am stunned. Dorothy embroiders the truth for the sake of emphasis, and though she has spoken occasionally of plastic surgery, I never believed her. She speaks to shock, and also, of course, I never believed her because I see no need for a facelift. Dorothy is young, or was then, a young forty.

"Why did you do it?" I shout at her. "You're falling for the myth. You looked fine before."

"I look terrible now," she says. "Come on over and bring some sherry. I need a glass."

"Seriously," I said, settling down opposite her chair in the rec room to pour sherry. "Did you do it to keep Mike attentive?"

It wasn't actually a serious question. It was more of a softening up, a beginning. Mike and Dorothy have been married since 1950. They have an amiable relationship that does not rely on how she—or he, for that matter—looks.

She looked like the victim of a street mugging. Both eyes

were black and swollen, and she seemed to fear to turn her head. Her whole face was puffy, mottled, and she appeared to be talking through a mask set in plaster.

"Mike?" she said between her teeth. "Mike? I did it because I couldn't stand looking in the mirror every morning at old me. Do you know that when I came out of the anesthetic I was wearing a helmet? What do you think that was for?"

"In case you are driven to butt your head against the wall," I told her. "Hold still while I take your picture. What did Mike say? Did you frighten him?"

"I don't think he noticed. He's very busy this week. Conference with the Seattle office."

"How old will this make you? Will it take off ten years?"

"They're careful what they promise, but it's supposed to hold up for five years." She now appeared to be speaking around a bit and bridle. "I expect to look ravishing. At least temporarily."

Next day I called back.

"I'm having your pictures developed," I said, "but in the meantime I have here this clipping that says that at the American Society of Aesthetic Plastic Surgery convention, in a survey of fifty female facelift patients, they found increased self-confidence and a tendency to be less inhibited in behavior and attire. God forbid that you should feel less inhibited. But you should, it says here, feel 'up.' Do you?"

Dorothy groaned.

"I hurt," she said.

Dorothy wasn't trying to please Mike, who in any case wouldn't notice, but bowing to the prevailing culture. Dorothy was simply trying to look younger. Dorothy was simply trying to look younger because—you hear it on the radio, see it on TV—the young have all the Fun and men fall in love with *young* women. Dorothy sends out messages that men find flattering, which has always disturbed me, but as my friend Mary points out, don't knock it; these are the ones that will be saved come the bomb, not the feminists. Step this way onto my raft, some surviving male will say, pushing off with his foot the frantic arms of ERA supporters. "How clever of you to find this old piece of roofing," Dorothy will say, hitching herself up to the makeshift raft and examining him to see if he's attractive.

Edith Wharton's Lily Bart worried when two little lines cropped up near her mouth. Oscar Wilde observed that a woman who will tell her age will tell anything. We have learned to keep our secrets, frizz our hair, and smile because men prefer young women or women who look young, and we don't want to lose out on the action. We play the game, knowing the rules are set.

Oh, husbands do it too, or baldness cures would drop from sight and they'd get their hair cut at the barber's the way they used to, instead of at a $20 stylist. But they don't get fired as talk show hosts for aging, and the proportion of women who run off with younger men must be minuscule or Mary Tyler Moore wouldn't have caused so much comment. It's okay for men to age. Look at Walter Cronkite and Burt Reynolds.

"The youth of America is their oldest tradition," observed Oscar Wilde tartly. "It has been going on now for 300 years." We women learn by osmosis the bias toward youth as the thirties arrive, from shifting male attention, from watching wives get younger and younger, from a thousand inarticulated messages from truck drivers and construction workers. Men prefer their women young. Youth is the ticket to the action. Men do not look twice at older women. For the aging there are retirement homes and bingo.

There are those who claim that the current fitness craze— the interest in jogging, health diets, and lunch hour workouts— is sweeping the country because the baby boom generation is staring in the mirror and beginning to see that growing older is, after all, a reality for everyone. "I'm not ready to look like my mother," screams Lois to the bathroom mirror in Lynn Johnston's *For Better or for Worse* comic strip. Younger people are nipping at the baby boom generation's heels, elbowing them out of the ads for condominiums and the better grades of whiskey, setting new fads in clothes and music. Teeny boppers are growing up and moving front and center. They said they were prepared to move off stage, but it's different now. "Hope I die before I get old," pulsed the rock of the sixties, but better yet, keep young.

A woman's job is to attract men, and to be suspected of having character is the kiss of death. It's clearly a woman's duty not to get past thirty if she wants to catch a man's eye.

Unless, of course . . .

The table around which we are sitting is dressed to kill. Hothouse flowers sit in a Sevres centerpiece, the crystal is hand cut. No one will mention it if you spill on the linen, but you would rather not for it is expensively elegant. Outside on the terrace the dogwoods are in full bloom, and beyond, the azaleas are trying to outdo each other. We are four women ranging from the mid-forties to the mid-sixties, and the subject is aging in women.

Everybody here is fashionably dressed and coiffed. Everybody but me is the wife of a highly successful, solvent man, mistress of a comfortable home. I want them to consider if there is a biological unfairness in the different way society judges the aging of men and women, but they have no complaints.

They shake their heads. "If you were alone, I guess it would be different," says one finally.

I keep worrying it. Doesn't a man have a more distinguished image with character lines and a touch of gray than a woman has? Supposing both are single; doesn't he cut more ice? Attract more attention than a woman of the same age?

"Not if she has money," says one of them. And the talk moves on.

"Men in their forties and fifties have a lot more to offer

than a woman has," says Dr. Pepper Schwartz, sociologist at the University of Washington and co-author of *American Couples*. "Like power and money."

Women are the ultimate realists, and they have observed how life works. It's okay to age if you've still got the husband you started with. Otherwise it's cold out there. They've noticed that.

Aurora Greenway, heroine of *Terms of Endearment*, gives us a straight look at fifty the way it is without a husband, fighting the years and building a wall of defenses against too high expectations. Jack Nicholson didn't look too great either, but he's making it nicely. The power structure is on his side.

There are plenty of voices out there confirming that the movie reflects things as they are and it's an uneven fight.

"In all countries women are more valued when they're pretty young things and still have their fertility," says Dr. Schwartz, who herself is still young and pretty. At Mt. Sinai Hospital Medical Center in New York City, Dr. Reun Tideksaar, a specialist in gerontology, says, "The culture has accepted the media message that the Pepsi generation is the model for us all."

"That's where the money is for advertising," says Dr. Tideksaar. "It's a youth market, and women are told that they must be pencil thin with unwrinkled skin. Nobody wants to grow old. We're all living by *Time*'s covers. We want to be what they claim everybody else is, young and sexy."

Facts are facts, and we trim our sails to the prevailing wind. But nearly everybody agrees that change may at last be lurking in the wings.

"We're seeing the seeds now," says Dr. Tideksaar. "The mean age is going up. Joan Collins is fifty and she was on the cover of *Playboy*. A cultural change in the perception of the older woman will come as surely as the change in the stigma on divorce. When I was growing up, it was terrible to go to school and have to say your parents were divorced. Now you're the odd one if you don't have four sets of grandparents."

"It's happening," agrees Dr. Schwartz.

"Yeah," says my friend Julia, who is forty-five, throwing herself on my sofa to contemplate the inequities of male and female aging. "They're looking for a cure for cancer too. It'll come with the millenium. I'm having my twenty-fifth college reunion this spring, and my reunion chairman began the funds drive letters, 'Dear girls.' We can't even grow up into women.

"Don't hold your breath."

The older a woman gets, the harder it is for her to find a husband. The odds go bad after twenty-four. We have it straight from the experts at Princeton.

In a study conducted by population researchers it was discovered that the only time the odds on finding a suitable mate are in the woman's favor is from twenty to twenty-four years.

But for white women twenty-five to twenty-nine there are only seventy-seven suitable men for every one hundred women. Suitability was defined as comparable age and education. For white women thirty to thirty-four the ration of husband material declined to sixty-two men to one hundred women. At every age after twenty-four a woman was at a disadvantage.

"Men are mostly married in their early thirties," says Liz, Joan's classmate, who is twenty-seven.

But Princeton population researcher Charles R. Hammerslough has another explanation.

"Men tend to marry women younger than themselves, while women who remarry tend to marry approximately the same age," he says.

Also working against a woman of twenty-four-plus, says Charles Westoff, director of population research for Princeton University, is the undeniable fact that most women don't want to marry younger men. We prefer to marry men older than we are.

"It's a cultural tradition to marry men two or three years older, a tradition rooted in the economic bargain. A man trades his money and status for a woman's child-bearing capabilities and domestic services. And this has led to women marrying older men.

"It's beginning to break down now that women are more economically self-sufficient. It's possible to imagine a society in which male and female are equal, and the age difference will disappear in marriage. But what I see is an increased number who will never marry and a continuing high divorce rate."

Randall Jarrell, in his poem "Next Day," puts a woman's ache for the days when "the world looks at me" into a poignant few lines.

> *When I was young and miserable and pretty*
> *And poor, I'd wish*
> *What all girls wish; to have a husband,*
> *A house and children. Now that I'm old, my wish*
> *Is womanish.*
> *That the boy putting groceries in my car*
> *See me. It bewilders me that he doesn't see me.*

He pats her dog instead, and with this realization, all the axioms, the laws of the universe that she knew did not apply to her, come true.

Once when Joan was still a basket case in something I think we called a baby-tote, I took her to the grocery store and plunked her, at the age of six weeks, wrapped in her blanket cocoon, into the shopping basket while I selected some fruit and vegetables.

The man weeding the tired produce from the more salable stopped his work briefly and gazed amiably down at her, smiling.

"Nice baby," he said. "Your grandchild?"

I was thirty-eight at the time, but my hair, like my mother's before me, was showing a wide white streak. I read the truth plain on this man's weatherbeaten countenance, this man to whom it has been entrusted to give the message. I might be Joan's mother, but I looked like her grandmother. Love and sex were beyond my reach; my hair was turning white.

I was not one at that point to take on crusades. I recognized immutable facts and had my hair dyed that day. I haven't flagged since.

Who is responsible for the culture's hang-up on youth? The experts point fingers at a variety of causes, but high on the list is always the advertising industry. If you drink that brand of scotch, use this brand of shampoo, you will look like these happy, vibrant young people in the picture. Compton Advertising, Inc., recently began to wonder just how young the optimum target is and turned up some odd facts. They asked 1,007 adults how old they were and how old they felt. They felt younger, it turned out, if they were financially comfortable, married, college-educated, and living in California. Middle-aged men, bucked up by society's view that they weather well as the years accumulate, felt five to fifteen years younger than the calendar said. Women of twenty to twenty-four, on the contrary, felt closer to thirty. Compton has announced they think "marketers might consider tailoring their products and advertising to people's perceived age as opposed to the traditional values and desires associated with their actual age." Most of the optimum targets fell into the thirty-to-thirty-five range. Not really young but carefully on the sunny side of forty.

Larry McMurtry, who created Aurora Greenway and is noted for his sensitivity to women no longer young, admits that there's a sociological unfairness in the way middle-aged men and women are viewed by the culture, but he doesn't think it's true that in any country middle-aged women are not valued. "I'm thinking of the Continent as a whole, where there is a certain mixture of all cultures," he says, "but there's a better balance there. It's changing here, but I don't know how long it will take to bring about a total reversal."

So then is it any wonder that we women are rushing to the plastic surgeons for help, spending billions on cosmetics, hair dyes, and reducing formulas?

"Men do it too," he points out, "but it's ridiculous in both cases. It's a stupid aspect of the culture to believe that the aging process can be cheated—no, that's the wrong word— belied."

He's speaking from his ranch in rural Texas, where his family lives and where he goes periodically to work on his novels.

"There's a general cultural loosening," he says. "They're more broad-minded right here than they were ten to fifteen years ago. As our society becomes more educated, it will be easier to run against the stereotypes."

There's a pause while he considers this, and then he volunteers that his twenty-two-year-old son has been living with a forty-two-year-old woman for three years. "They have no difficulty introducing each other to their friends. My own romances have been with women in their forties and fifites. I'm somewhat optimistic."

But will women really marry younger men? Will we shake the dependent role and break that tradition?

Yes, says Dr. Pepper Schwartz, whose theory is that women marrying younger men will answer the problem of the women of the baby boom generation. Right now in fourteen percent of the marriages the man is younger, pretty unusual fifty years ago.

How nice it would be if Dr. Schwartz turns out to be right, because a woman of thirty has a hard time playing the same game as her male peers who are looking at a woman of perhaps twenty. To a man of forty-two, this woman looks young, but so does that same twenty-year-old woman on which her male peers are focusing. And there aren't many forty-two-year-old men compared to the number of women in the baby boom generation because they were born in wartime when the men were overseas and babies scarce.

"I think of the men who interest me as forty-five to sixty," says my friend Eileen. "Ironically, my peers don't look in their own age group for female company. They're trying to find youth by dating young."

She is editing a travel piece of mine, but the laws of the universe often creep into our conversations.

"This hardly comes as news, Eileen. I'll listen better when you tell me it's changing."

"It will," she says confidently. "It's not with it anymore to refer to women as girls."

"Yeah? One small step for womankind. You can't fight city hall."

"It will change when our identities range beyond 'wife of.' Once we're not positioned by history and economics in the role of heifers at the county fair, with prospective buyers going mainly on the exterior package, it will change."

"I must introduce you to some sociologists I know," I tell her.

"Don't men depreciate? How about that bald spot and the paunch? But that wouldn't stop me from falling for a man. Age afflicts both men and women."

"Don't complain to me. I'm a convinced audience."

Dr. Ehrenreich, the respected student of women's changing status, is forty-two, and she says flatly she intends to help improve the cultural bias against middle-aged women.

She's feeling encouraged that not every Hollywood leading lady is twenty these days, that Jane Fonda is not yet a character actress, that Gloria Steinem is fifty. Candice Bergen is in her late thirties.

These are small portents, she admits, but she remembers

that Marilyn Monroe was thirty-six when she took too many pills, maybe partially because of her fear that she was over the hill.

"We've been changing a lot of things that were once considered 'natural,' things taken for granted by earlier societies. Think of birth control. There's no need to live with primitive ideas."

But she also thinks that how the world assesses a woman depends on who the woman is. "A professor of English is probably doing her best work in middle age. Maybe the experience of being a housewife for twenty years doesn't leave you a very interesting person. To be so narrowed down, within four walls. I don't know.

"But men who leave middle-aged women for younger ones probably do it for much simpler reasons," she says. "The contempt for the aging woman will change only when women get more power. I worry about displaced homemakers. A deep sense of dignity and self-respect rests on work."

"I shall never be old enough to forget love and to stop thinking about it, and talking about it," said Collette, who was only nineteen when she married Willy, her tyrannical and much older husband. Brave words, but for most women today a mockery.

Dr. Andrew Hacker of Queens College, who describes himself as a sociologist, demographer, even psychologist-manqué packaged as a social scientist ("though I'd rather not be caught on a desert island with one"), is blunt about the realities.

"None of this sounds very nice," he says, "but a woman has roughly the years between seventeen and twenty-seven before she is depreciated like an automobile. Young women don't look ahead; the future never comes, and the statistics that show remarriage possibilities are deceiving. We're told that three-quarters of women remarry after divorcing, but that's bullshit. If she divorces after three or four years, she gets remarried, but the first wasn't really marriage. More of a steady date.

"After thirty-seven, her chances of remarriage plummet."

It's the old story. The first time, the man marries a woman about a year and a half younger. By the time he's forty he wants a woman ten-plus years younger, says Dr. Hacker, who also has noticed something else interesting. His wife, he says, works with some very successful women. "The men won't look at them. They're not interested even if the women listen well. Listening well he can get more pleasantly from a younger woman."

It's curious, thinks Dr. Hacker, that the young feminists in their thirties choose to hook up with men who are stronger and more powerful than they. The men they meet know all the word games about equality between the sexes, keeping up with the trends as they work out in the gyms flattening their stomachs, but the feminists are looking for more.

I could have told Dr. Hacker that. A woman can maybe look levelly at a man, though never down, but what she secretly wants, feminist or not, is to look up. She might compromise if she's in bad financial or emotional straits, but that's what she'd like.

And now, Dr. Hacker, what about the inequality in aging? Will the culture change?

"In two hundred years, maybe. A big fat maybe."

At this Fourth of July picnic I am the only one you could call middle-aged. We sit around the park table/bench heaped high with fried chicken, deviled eggs, fruit, cheese, and brownies, elbows on the table, drinking wine from paper cups. A small boy belonging to the people at the next table has joined us to throw the ball for Katy, and the July sun is hot on our backs.

On my right, Liz, just back from visiting her family in New York, is saying vehemently, "They think I'll be pleased, but I'm not. It bothers me."

What bothers her is the constant murmur of relatives, seeing her for the first time in several years, remarking on how pretty she is. At twenty-seven, Liz has lovely clear white skin, big black eyes fringed with lashes that look too heavy to lift, and the fresh appeal of every young woman in her twenties. It's hard not to be pretty at twenty-seven.

"Why do you mind?" I want to know, stuffing down another brownie.

She searches in her mind for the reasons why she is put off by compliments.

"They didn't say that when I was a teenager, and it makes you wonder what they'll say when I'm forty. It's not me they're complimenting."

I am stunned. Is it possible that sometimes we do see it coming, even when we're not yet thirty?

What if we women did flout the statistics and our inclinations and dip into the pool of younger men for husbands? How would it work? The *Washingtonian* magazine posed this question to a fifty-year-old divorcée television producer who considered briefly and shot back, "Imagine waking up in the morning with someone who didn't know who Adlai Stevenson was?"

Liz Carpenter, Ladybird Johnson's press secretary and a widow, says a gap of more than five years would make her uncomfortable. Her solution to the shrinking pool of marriageable men for single women is to convert the gays. "They're so handy at dinner parties."

Of course, marrying younger men is one thing for a woman in her fifties and quite another at thirty. Or is it?

We're sitting, the four of us, on an enclosed porch looking out over the garden of a suburban house, gathered to eat what has become known as the Colonel's scallops, and to pass a summer evening. The Colonel who loves to cook and is splendid at it, finds it boring not to have someone to put his creations in front of. Tonight his grandson and his wife are with him, paying a not infrequent visit to keep him company, and I have been invited to join them.

We are talking of husbands and age, of men and women, and how life treats us severally and generally. Faith tells me she is five years older than her husband.

She's wearing a becoming dress cut low in the back, and the very way she sits in her rattan chair tells you she is accustomed to catching the eye of men. She's been helping the Colonel plant his tomato plants and is worried about an allergy she thinks is marring the skin around her eyes, an allergy totally imperceptible to anyone else.

She's thirty and clearly very pretty, a fortuitous mix of Mexican and Irish that has produced spunk as well as charm.

"I married younger," she says, "and I'm afraid of what's going to happen."

There he sits, ten feet away, her husband of three years, a twenty-five-year-old Army captain, clean cut, good looking, well-mannered, regarding her silently.

"He looks them up and down every day," she says. "He fantasized about my best friend. I knew it, and he admitted it. I could do that. Walk through the officers' club and look them over, but I'd feel demeaned."

Her eyes were flashing, but her husband still says nothing, eyeing her perfect face with the arched eyebrows and flawless skin as if it reflected someone else's peccadilloes. He looks neither disturbed nor concerned. He does not deny what she says.

Once she was in the army too, but when they were married she didn't reenlist. She works in a civilian job now and hopes they will be transferred overseas. She thinks it would be exciting. This is no housewife, building her life on the moment when he comes home from duty. She's plain-spoken and her voice counts in the marriage. You can tell that.

"Why do men need variety?" she demands of no one in particular, and her voice is angry. "Why isn't one woman enough?" She does not look at me.

"Is this an old army tradition?" I ask her husband. "Macho among the boys?" In the corner the Colonel, a product of West Point and a remarkably young and vigorous man, stirs in his chair. He is not averse to recalling his conquests. Rank has its privileges.

"Maximum opportunity, maybe," says his grandson.

He was not her first husband. She was married at seventeen to a boy of twenty. Her mother told her that the sex bit came with the deal. She was surprised that it was no burden. She had one child. "When you marry, you have children," she says. They got divorced and she enlisted. The child stayed with her mother.

"We were too young," she says flatly. "We didn't know who we were."

Her new husband has risen fast. Twenty-five is young to be a captain. He looks dashing in his Green Beret uniform. He already has a company under his command.

What could he want with more woman than this pretty, outspoken, angry wife of his?

"It's the ego," she says. "I'm afraid of what will happen."

Dr. Estelle Ramey, an endocrinologist at Georgetown University, deliberately wears ruffles when she lectures and tells her audience early on she's a grandmother.

"How could a grandmother be abrasive?" she inquires sweetly. Then she lets 'em have it. Dr. Ramey is an angry woman.

Women, she says, are valued for youth and beauty, which are ephemeral; men are valued for money and power which aggrandize. Only rich women escape devaluation as they age. "It's been that way for thousands of years," she says, "and women have been compliant with the idea. In primitive societies man was the larger animal and not in danger of getting pregnant. If power corrupts, then men have been corrupted by absolute power.

"The game-playing between men and women is fun, amusing, sexy, but it can be costly," she says. "It undervalues women."

Strength in women has not been admired by men or by women. On every hand you hear it threatens femininity. Legion are the women who have drawn back for fear of what overwhelming success could do to their private lives, the ego of males in their lives. He, of course, is boldly aggressive; she is pushy. He is decisive; she is opinionated. He is strong; she is abrasive.

Such talk annoys Dr. Ramey.

"Strength," she says crisply, "is the ability to forestall ravages. And as for femininity, it's yours for life, by birth."

It's especially interesting, she thinks, that we don't see middle-aged women standing shoulder to shoulder on this. Women who take their identity from a man see strength in other women as denigrating their own dependence. They may see the feminists as abrasive. Women, she thinks, are in competition for the gold wedding ring in the same way men compete for the vice-presidency. The single exception was the pioneer woman who helped other women in a world their husbands ruled.

Maybe strength comes best from the fire, and if there's no need to struggle, you don't get tempered. I thought about this when I met Madeline Landing Potts, a forty-one-year-old grandmother from Winter Park, Florida.

I met Madeline at a crafts show where she was exhibiting beautiful hand-turned pots she made in her pottery business back in Florida. Business was slow, and we sat down together for a moment because she is friendly, and I like to hear about other people's lives.

She didn't look forty-one. Her hair was fashionably frizzy, and she wore sandals and loose, floating clothes I'm more accustomed to seeing on people in their twenties.

"That name came from my business," she said, showing

me her card. "After my divorce I thought how my identity was in my business, so I just took it for my name too. So now my business is me."

I suppose we got on the subject of growing older because she was so young to be a grandmother. Her face lit up when she told me about her grandson. She helped deliver him and made the occasion a family festival. As the grandmother, she felt she had contributed something. She said she looked forward to being an old lady.

Look *forward* to being an old lady?

But youth is everything, Madeline. You with the young-looking body, how could you wish for more years that can only bring trouble, infirmities, less esteem, difficulties, fewer chances at love?

Craft shows attract the young, and all around us couples are milling, studying woven serapes, pewter vases, kaleidoscopes, dried flowers, herbs, jewelry. Madeline looks around her as if the answer lies somewhere in the crowd, and then she rests her chin in her hand and tells me what she has discovered since her divorce.

What she has discovered is that even at thirty she didn't know who she was.

"I suppose," she says in her gentle voice, "that people at eighteen and twenty now find it easier than I did to find out that they are somebody, but I was still learning my identity at thirty. It's a growth process. Oh, I see funny things happening to my body. But my mind is stronger, and I have more to offer than I did when I was younger. I learn something every day. I feel great about my age."

A customer seeks her out to buy one of her pots, and she takes the money almost abstractedly.

"You know," she says, "at shows like this you get little rushes of sympathy and love, talking to people who tell you major feelings right out. People's concerns are really very universal. I think it's sad that everybody thinks they should be young. Maybe I won't be able to drag my display around the way I do now when I'm older, but I'll hire someone to do it. I'll do it. It's a matter of spirit. You know, I worry about the details in a show like this—the car breaking down, things like that—but when I've managed to do it, it's such a wonderful feeling.

"I know who I am now."

Now if we could only bottle some of this and sell it right there on the counter beside the hair dyes.

Chapter

11

*Home for Lunch
Forever*

I married him for better or worse, goes the old saying, but not for lunch. And all of a sudden, after spending 70 percent of his time at work, a husband is a live-in constant companion. It requires quite a shift in thinking.

Moreover, if we can believe a 1981 Louis Harris survey, most Americans in all age groups don't look forward to retiring, and nearly half of those already retired didn't look forward to stopping work. What we have are husbands (and they are mostly husbands, since women didn't enter the work force in sizable enough numbers early enough to be currently retired) who are not too happy with 100 percent leisure and not particularly equipped to deal with it. This is not true universally, but it's true enough to cause consternation.

Charles Lamb wrote about the trauma of retirement nearly 150 years ago.

"For the first day or two I felt stunned, overwhelmed, I could only apprehend my felicity; I was too confused to taste it sincerely. I wandered about thinking I was happy, and knowing that I was not. I was in the condition of a prisoner in the old Bastille, suddenly let loose after 40 years' confinement. I could scarcely trust myself with myself. It was like passing out of Time into Eternity—for it is a sort of Eternity for a man to have his Time all to himself.

"I missed my old chains," said Lamb. "Having all holidays, I am as though I had none."

The shock waves that radiate from twentieth-century reflections of Lamb's rude awakening have caused some rethinking in many marriages. Fear begins in the fifties and builds as the moment for the golden handshake, the farewell pat on the back, approaches.

"Bill was sick last week," says a golfing companion of mine, "and when he improved, he stood over me with advice on everything. I'm not loading the dishwasher efficiently; the thermostat is too high; the laundry cycle is wrong. When he retires, I'll lose my mind."

At loose ends, with enforced leisure, Bill was intruding into my friend's world, a world of which she has been sole captain for years. This marriage will survive it, but many feel the strain. The moment of truth looms for every marriage, excepting only those in which the husband works for himself. In 1900, four out of five men were still working after sixty-five; today it is one out of five.

In America work identifies. It's what the fencing is about at cocktail parties. "What do you do?" is just another way of asking the unaskable, "Who are you?" It's the same question, and everybody knows it. "You're lucky," a newly retired man wrote me. "You have an identifiable reason for living. I feel I'm at the end of my life."

Men especially suffer from the removal of this identification. Men's friends are friends of the road. They played football together at college or golf on weekends after they were married, or especially they worked together in the same company. And with one torn page of the calendar office friends disappear. Oh, there'll be occasional lunches, but office friends still employed are *busy*.

Golf is left. Golf is a leisure sport, and leisure is what a retired husband has in large quantity. Golf is the saving grace, easier than tennis for an older man—at least until a knee goes bad or arthritis takes its toll. Even if you pick up and settle in those heavenly waiting rooms, the retirement communities where *nobody* works, you can't count on playing golf forever.

Whom does this leave? Why your wife, of course. A built-in companion who seems to have figured out her life quite well. Where is she going this morning? Why not go along with her?

Lynn Jafsinger is a newish friend of mine, picked up quite literally, because Lynn is friendly and opens conversations with strangers on whim. She was eating a chicken sandwich and annointing herself with perfumed suntan lotion when I passed by her table at the golf club. She had never seen me before, but she invited me to sit down if I was alone. I was and I did, and we've been friends ever since.

Getting caught up on our preacquaintance life, I learned she was born in Manhattan, had worked for a while for *Life* magazine, and was married to a Foreign Service officer, now retired.

I asked her how this worked out, since Foreign Service officers seem to enjoy being citizens of the world.

She worked assiduously at applying the lotion.

"We were Siamese twins," she said crossly. My mayonnaise seemed to smell of the lotion, and I moved my plate farther out of range. "At the end of the day when we sat down for dinner, we had nothing to say to each other. I went out and got a job."

Left alone, her husband developed his own avocations, possibly not meaningful but adequate. To the library to read *The Wall Street Journal*. The library is four blocks away, a nice walk, so doubly pleasant. An occasional lunch with an old colleague. A stop at the fruit-and-vegetable man. Eventually, he had a life.

Winston Copeland was also a Foreign Service officer after a stint with UPI, and he too retired early. Now when his wife, Anne, gives a luncheon party for women, he helps cook, bartends, and when it's time to eat, joins the party.

"After helping get it, what else?" he says, reclining comfortably against sofa cushions. "Roy Rogers?"

He cooks, gardens, and reads and is clearly happy. "I like quiet," he says comfortably. "UPI was hectic and Foreign Service is a twenty-four-hour-a-day job."

Cope, as his friends call him, has fallen into a retirement that works for him, but not everyone is so lucky.

"I miss the companionship of men," says Harold Eisen, a retired General Motors personnel officer now living in Grand Rapids. He's a widower and divorced from his second wife, and he has no trouble finding female companionship, but the close support of the men he worked with is missing. He solves this on the golf course, playing in all of the seniors' tournaments, where he meets men looking for the same companionship, making connections with others who have also shucked the job for the world without clocks. He went back to his college reunion and to the reunion of his fighter pilot squadron. He reads regularly to a shut-in blind man and is big on Meals on Wheels.

" 'Retire,' of course, is a polite synonym for retreat," says my brother-in-law, a tall lean Texan who spent most of his life in state government in Austin.

For Orus—my mother-in-law started out thinking she'd give all the children names that began with O—retirement was "a retreat from a time of usefulness. It changed for me my feelings of worthiness. I had attained a position where my advice was sought and respected. At retirement I had to abandon all of that pretty much."

The worst was the total freedom.

"The requirements of work bring a certain orderliness that is addictive. Such habits are hard to break. There is much to be said for a comfortable rut, and rolling free at the end of it is destabilizing."

And Helen, his wife? So close is this marriage that Orus cannot even sign a letter with his name alone.

"Like most husbands I suppose I was inclined to blame my retirement on my wife instead of on my age, probably because she didn't seem to be suffering from it as much as I."

Faced with a whole world of leisure, some prefer to seek the structured life, an unexamined life of all play, in the retirement communities. Retirement community planners have fattened on this new leisure class. Bingo in the evening, lawn bowling in the morning, arts and crafts in the community center all day long, and classes to teach you how. It seems particularly right that these places are usually put down in the land of eternal summer. Reality, even of the seasons, is kept nicely at bay. Three out of four who bought this idea love it, say Gordon L. Butena and Vivian Wood, who collaborated on an examination of these single-age communities.

Retired Colonel Arthur and Florence Flestito gave their furniture to their children, cut their eastern ties, and moved west to Tucson about three years ago. Arthur, who had been retired for some time, loved and manicured the garden of his eastern home, and I wondered how he would make out, since there was to be no garden, no private land in the Arizona apartment complex. They had been neighbors of mine for years, and I paid them a call to say good-bye. I hate good-byes, and this was the worst kind. The furniture had largely departed the living room, and I felt they were gone already.

"We're just going to pick up and go," said Florence in her usual little breathless rush of words. "I have a sister out there."

I could hear the tightness of her voice, wondering what they had opted for.

Not long ago I called them in Arizona. Florence answered. Arthur was out playing golf.

I wanted to know if he missed his garden.

Her voice was light and cheerful.

"He wouldn't garden now if he had one," she said. "This place is just right for him. He even has walk-in friends."

What about her?

"I took up tennis," she says. "I play four times a week. I took lessons, and I have lots of partners. Now he goes his way and I go mine, and we meet at five o'clock for the happy hour."

What kind of people?

"Twenty out of a hundred of these apartment complexes are for permanent residents like us. It's like a resort hotel, a vacation that never ends. I gave everything to my children and started over. It's like playhouse living. Easy upkeep and definitely less money."

I am thinking that there seem to be no holes in this life of all play, no work, no worry, and there are holes in everything. Am I getting the party line?

"Oh, the holes are that I don't get to see the children. But now I'm Florence. I'm me. Before I felt very old; now I'm starting over."

There's a pause while we both mull this over.

"Right now," she says, "I'm looking at the mountains, and they're so beautiful. It's all perfect."

They're not the only ones who talk like this. Let me introduce you to the Joffees.

I knew Ann Joffee when we were both in our twenties. I haven't seen her for a long time now, but if we met we'd have no trouble talking. That's a tribute to Ann, who is easy with people. When we were growing up, her telephone was busy with calls from boys who liked that warm obligatto of chatter at picnics, over a glass of beer, on the way to the movies. Leave Ann alone with a mountaintop hermit, and when you came back you'd find the two of them rocking comfortably on his front porch and nattering away cozily.

She got married, and I got married and moved to Dallas, and so we didn't meet very often; and when I last saw her we had a lot of catching up to do. Ed Joffee is retired now, at a very young age because of a corporate merger, and I asked her how retirement was going.

"Wonderful," she said at once. "Ed played golf eleven out of the last twelve days. Three times a week with me and the rest with the men."

"He's happy?"

"He's happy. I'm happy. We're doing what we want to do."

Can a man be happy totally isolated from the work world, devoting 100 percent of his time to pleasure? "To be idle is to become a stranger unto the seasons and to step out of life's procession," said Kahlil Gabran. Duke Ellington put it a little differently. "Retired people," he said, "lie under a tree and play checkers, and the first thing you know, they're gone." Best of all, as far as I'm concerned, was Senator Claude Pepper's comment: "Life is like riding a bicycle. You're all right as long as you keep pedaling."

I have trouble believing that total play is enough after a life of work that matters.

"It's not," says E. Bentley Lipscomb, minority staff director of the Senate Special Committee on Aging. "People can do this play business just so long."

Lipscomb was part of a study investigating this point under Senator John Childs of Florida, and what floated to the surface was that most of the retirees, given their druthers, would prefer to be working still. But then, of course, like Lipscomb's own father, they had no choice in the matter most of the time.

His father was a busy South Carolina accountant when at sixty-five he got the gold watch. He went into a total decline so pronounced that, though Lipscomb lived eight hundred miles away, his mother called him to come talk with his father.

"He had talked himself into a psychosomatic illness," says Lipscomb. "He had an underlying heart problem, but it was never going to carry him off. With nothing to do he convinced himself he was sick. I had to pick him up and dump him into a hospital, where his internist ordered a battery of tests with the understanding that, if nothing serious showed up, he would walk out of there and do something with his life. His doctor told him straight out he was in a prison of his own making."

Nothing was wrong, and Lipscomb senior, reassured, went out and got part-time work helping people prepare their income taxes. This keeps him busy through April 15 every year, and at seventy-three he has added work with an auctioneer, keeping books. Today he is happy and healthy, and his wife sighs with relief.

The rest of the day after I talked to Lipscomb I was haunted with memories of my own father. He was eighty-two when my brother and my aunties got together to vote him out of the presidency of the family business.

I pass no judgment on whether or not the company economically prospered from the ousting. All I know is, as a widower, my father had made that company his life. He was not only the president but the man who mailed the letters on the way home, locked up the safe, and watered the plants.

Before the vote one of my aunties called me to ask for Booth's and my advice.

"If they do that, your father will be dead in two weeks," said Booth.

They did it, and my father was dead in ten days. You can't take away a man's reason for living and expect him to survive.

I told this story to Isabelle Claxton, who works as a press aide on the majority side of the Special Committee for Aging.

"My father," she said, "had a total personality change when he was forced to retire from the Foreign Service at sixty.

"Work was his hobby. He didn't play golf or tennis. He had this pension that would have kept him and my mother nicely, but he didn't care. He wanted my mother to join a square dance group, to go out all the time with him—all totally out of character. She felt rather threatened, because her life was just the same as it had always been, but he was obviously wrestling with overpowering demons.

"He wrestled with it all for four months and then he went out and got a job. He was terribly afraid he was too old, because everybody else was in their late thirties or early forties, but he brought great expertise to the job and they hired him. Now he travels all over the world for the group interested in population control. He's even learned computers."

"But your mother," I said. "She doesn't travel all over the world with him, does she?" I had visions of her with her worst fears realized, a husband doing what he wants to do but not where she is.

"That's the exciting thing," says Claxton. "She's sixty-five and she's never worked in her life, but now she's started a tour group that takes people through the Hebrides. And they're both happy."

A shining success story, but not everybody is ready for these new ventures. Some find retirement an experience that destroys their identity. The bookstores are full of how-to books with upbeat advice on how to handle this inevitable rite of passage—upbeat books with cheerful titles. It is fashionable now to look ahead to the retirement years, to plan for them.

Dr. Curtis Moore was dean of the evening and summer sessions at Rockford College in Illinois until he retired in 1979. Now he's teaching courses in the art of retirement at the college. He's teaching men in their fifties, men looking ahead to what they'll do with their lives in their seventies. His wife teaches a class too, and she constantly finds wives apprehensive about the retirement years, thinking of their husbands under foot all day long with no real purpose to their days.

The Moores live in a cottage duplex on the grounds of a retirement home, and the advice they give comes from close understanding and observation.

When I talked to Dr. Moore, I began with a personal broadside. What has the teacher himself learned? Earlier I had inquired of Mrs. Moore about this, and she gave him a good report. I wondered how he felt.

"When I retired I had Kiwanis and the Boy Scouts, which kept my friendships warm," he told me. Even though he doesn't pack up and chaperone camping trips anymore, he's still on the board, still in touch. He doesn't point out that this gives him some feeling that he matters, but this comes through without words. He says it obliquely when he tells me how the women in his retirement community meet every Monday to do craft work to be sold for the benefit of the health unit.

"Something for somebody else," he says. "And of course the chatter is important too."

His students, men whose retirement is maybe ten years off, come in "absolutely blank scared." He tells them that every day they must have a fresh commitment. Some reason for getting up.

"I tell 'em they and their wives must have separate lives and meet for lunch with something to talk about. And I especially tell 'em not to let the children make them into baby-sitters. I tell 'em to make it plain that both they and their wives have scheduled lives and daily commitments, and they are not free to care for the baby right now."

Dr. Moore laments that the cohesive family of 1900 is fragmented by the high-rise mobility of the eighties. The high-rises have decentralized people and made it even harder on people losing business friends. Men, says Dr. Moore, need social relations, and they're harder to come by these days. In a high-rise you don't lean over the garden fence and discuss the barking of the dog in the next block, the raccoon in the trash, the daily business of life.

The Moores are living what they preach, and they take time to look around them. They've noticed a couple that lives nearby, a retired vice-president of a large corporation and his wife. In this couple it is the wife who has trouble with her husband's retirement.

"They sold all their silver and china before they arrived," says Dr. Moore. "They never cook a meal. She looks all day long at television. He, on the other hand, is reaching out for new connections, stops to chat when he meets people on the street. Often," says the doctor, oblivious to the myths shattering about his head, "it is the retired husband who is concerned with the wife's happiness and health, but it doesn't work the other way."

Often?

"Oh, you and I both know people who are different, but by and large."

Dr. Moore is, in a way, a soldier in the fight to keep community ties intact for retired men. He's helping to push the trend, just starting in corporations and the federal government, to bring retired men back into the office in various roles. AID, the Agency for International Development, regularly brings back their retired employees to screen new applicants for the agency. Sunstrand, an aviation firm; J. L. Clark, a can manufacturing firm; and Camcar Textron are all experimenting with retired employees in the office to share retirement wisdom.

"It's a help," says Dr. Moore, "if they think about it before sixty-five minus one day. It takes planning."

In Kansas another doctor who retired in 1976 is also thinking about how to keep the peace in a home that a wife has been running alone until the day when her husband no longer goes to work. Dr. Don Carlos Peete, with fifty-one years of medicine behind him, divides his time these days between a home in Madeira Beach, Florida, and a new townhouse he and his wife, Alice, traded in for their big old house in Overland Park.

"Sure, a man with leisure gets impatient," says Dr. Peete, who sounds as if he is the most patient of men. "He sees things that should be done, eyesores I call them. They're things that bother you that you see ought to be done around the house and garden. I was raised with a father who had a lot of eyesores. My son didn't have any at first, but he developed them."

Alice Peete is not for a moment admitting that her husband troubled her with his eyesores. "I'm more of a perfectionist than he is," she says stoutly. "But lots of the patients' wives told me that they'd looked forward to their husbands' retirement for years, and it turned out to be difficult. So many were used to schedules.

"He has his golf. I can't play anymore. I have this trouble with my knee. I used to play with him. Now I drool every time I pass a course."

Dr. Peete says only that when ladies retire they keep around them the things they had around them most of their lives. A man, he thinks, needs good things to take him out of the house. He has to have something to do.

"If I don't play golf, I try to take a walk. You have to keep busy, develop a new interest in things, maybe gardening or finance, get an increased knowledge of trees. Some of the people I play golf with don't take time to look at the trees. You have to learn patience and not to be troubled."

"Alice," bellows Harry Frollicker, the husband of a friend of mine, home from work with a bad back. "That machine is *overloaded*. You'll make the motor burn out. And when is the last time you had Bertha clean the oven? It smells funny."

In three years Harry will retire. Alice Frollicker is afraid she can't stand up under his perfectionism.

Maybe some of us have trouble with the idea of retirement because it's official notice of old age's arrival. I keep thinking of Catherine Gallagher, a widow accountable to no one and a noted expert in the field of adolescent sex, who has worked in a subcabinet position in every administration from Roosevelt to Nixon. She officially retired during Nixon's administration, but not so you'd notice it. Her wellspring of energy would do credit to the age group she's concerned with, and she sat on advisory committees long after her retirement, not to mention writing a book.

We were sitting in her beautiful old country farmhouse in Virginia on a spring evening that made the Blue Ridge, hazy on the horizon, look purple.

"I'm really retiring at last," she tells me. "Selling the place, winding up the loose ends, and moving to a California retirement home."

I was shocked.

"Why ever would you do that? Leave the horses and the dogs and your son?"

"My son's going to be stationed abroad. I'm taking one of the horses." The dogs she carefully did not mention. Or the Persian cat that stalks majestically about the place. "I suppose there's always a catalyst. It was the IRS that did it."

She drained her cup and put it carefully on the table.

"They're auditing me. I had to dig out all these boxes of records that I couldn't lift. So I called Albert, you know, who rented the gatehouse, to come and help me—it's part of the deal. And his wife came along too, and she looked at all those papers and then at me, and she said, 'I don't think it's nice for the government to bother old people like this.' "

"To the young, thirty is getting on," I said comfortingly, but she ignored me.

"And I saw," she said, "that all this time I thought I was projecting an image of great self-sufficiency, a widow really meeting the challenge, making it on her own, but all the time I was just projecting 'old.' "

"But what will you do?" I asked her, still shocked. "Work is your life. Why are you doing this?"

"I've made a list," she said. "Here."

There in her indecipherable scrawl was a list of reasons why she was relinquishing a lifelong involvement in her work. With some help from her, I puzzled it out.

relief from accomplishment
Mr. Updike
time to watch the tomato plants grow
Learning that time is not so costly that it can't be wasted on trivia
learning that I value time slipping away and enjoy sunsets more
time for reflection (I'm reading my husband's diaries. I never permitted myself pleasure in the past before)
time to nap without guilt

I studied it and felt a lump in my throat.

"Mr. Updike?"

"Oh, well, he won't be my neighbor anymore, but he's symbolic. He used to drop in. Drop in and chat. He was a nice man, but I was always impatient that he consumed so much of my time."

I handed the list back to her. "Maybe you're doing the right thing," I said.

She packed up and went out to Carmel. She sent me pictures of incredibly beautiful grounds and of herself standing in front of her duplex, smiling into the sun. A postcard followed.

"I'm working on the idea that we could have a community dog," it said in the familiar scrawl. A card from Catherine is a week-long pleasure like a crossword puzzle. "I've made friends and we all meet for cocktails. They call us the jet set."

I keep mulling it over in my mind—the total happiness of the golfers and the body blows absorbed by my father and the fathers of Lipscomb and Claxton. And the shattering moment when Catherine Gallagher looked up from her work and found that she was old. And I see that there is no common thread, no rule, because it depends on who you are.

And most especially it depends on what your work means to you and how much of a hole laying it down leaves in your life, how much you must depend on those around you to fill the gap—which may be why some plunge into retirement like a warm bubble bath and some just turn up their toes and die.

Across the table a woman leans forward to tell us about her visit with her husband to a resort community favored by well-to-do retirees.

"They were glad to see us," she says emphatically. "A break in the routine."

Routine?

"Up bright and early in the morning for eighteen holes and lunch at the club. Then, for the young-old, tennis; for the middle age-old who don't play tennis, more golf. Then to whoever's turn it is for cocktails, but nobody stays late, of course. Got to get up early in the morning for the tee-off."

Bridge, of course, if it rains.

"They've all made it," she explains. "They don't need to worry about anything."

For some of us the end of the working years means only a choice of where to settle to spend the pension, where the leisure activities are best. But the end of work that held the real meaning of life, work that must be given up because of the infirmities of age, is different. It affects a man differently, and the woman he married as well. Follow me up these three flights of stairs. We're paying a visit to Phip, a caddy of mine for many years and before me, when he was a young buck fresh from the Carolinas, a tournament caddy, the epitome of the sport, a favorite of Walter Hagen. "I had a good eye and a quiet mouth," he says. That, of course, was before electric carts.

That's Phip waiting in the lobby, leaning on his cane. His knee has gone bad on him, but his unfailing courtesy nevertheless brings him down the stairs to greet guests.

You have to knock three times and wait and knock once more when you come to Phip's apartment. Phip's wife, Lucy, won't open the door otherwise. Hoodlums are not unknown in this building, and they are not swayed by the "God Is Love" sign on the door.

If you're a guest in Phip's apartment, you sit on the edge of the bed, which is in the living room, the only room heated enough to sit in in winter. Over the bed is a big picture of Franklin D. Roosevelt and one of Jesus. The space heater hums away cozily.

Last time I was here I asked Phip about his retirement. Caddies don't get Social Security, and he never complains, but I know things must get tight even though Lucy worked briefly during World War II and thus draws a small check. Where the rest comes from it's hard to imagine.

"I never did really retire," says Phip. "I'll be out there again."

Lucy looks on silently, her thin knees covered by a shawl. Nothing is clearer than that in this small room the country club and the fairways and the manicured greens are a palpable presence still. When I come I tell Phip how the fairways are this season, and he listens closely. In the face of the phalanx of electric carts Phip and I continued to walk those fairways until he was almost the last caddy to show up.

The small space heater spits a bit and I think that, however tight the money, these two survivors have each other and would get along somehow. Two together are better than one—where is it in the Bible that if one falls the other will hold him up?—and it never counts more than in a marriage. They looked at me politely, and I considered saying this, but then I thought they probably knew it.

"I'll call you next summer when the weather's warm," I say instead. "We might go nine holes."

Everybody knew this wasn't going to happen, but we felt better that I had said it.

'It's hard for people looking at the problem from their own perspective to see that whereas their own work is central to their lives, most people retire as soon as possible to get away from work that is demeaning. If they retire voluntarily, they do very well. That's if they're not sick. Sick retirees don't do well. Sick people die," says Dr. Barry Lebowitz, a psychiatrist concerned with gerontology at the National Institute of Mental Health.

So much for Charles Lamb and his missed chains, for Lipscomb's father and Claxton's father. Dr. Lebowitz goes even further. "Rarely does retirement put a strain on the marriage," he says, "though data are beginning to come in that point to the probability that two-income marriages suffer because the man's work history is longer and he's eligible for retirement earlier and wants to travel."

What about work identifying, Dr. Lebowitz?

"Only in Washington," he says, and he's very sure. "The rest of the country doesn't care."

He cites the example of the Detroit assembly-line worker. Does a man who inserts one screw in a body assembly think of his job as identifying him? No, Dr. Lebowitz. He probably thinks of himself as a Tiger-booster. Clearly, it's all a matter of what your work means to you, or meant to you before you quit. And who you are and if you have ingrained in you that you must contribute something to life. And if the marriage can stand a turning back onto its own resources.

And also, of course, it has something to do with how you perceive yourself.

Economist John Kenneth Galbraith, writing in *The New York Times Book Review* about the corporate management man and his retirement, makes it clear that the cost of surrender to the corporation in return for pay, stock options, golden parachutes, benefits, and other perks may well come due on retirement and its effect ripple outward to wives, families, and friends.

"There should be treatment [in literature] of the day of the terrible first death which comes with the announcement that the executive is 'taking early retirement' and his discovery that banality unbacked by the name of General Motors or Citibank has no audience. Then eventually the second death, at most a couple of weak paragraphs in the *Times*."

Are there any answers? How can a man prepare himself for the loss of identity and the 100 percent leisure of no work? Or do husbands handle the huge change in their lives for better or worse according to their own resources, inner and financial, and the support of those around them?

"Guesses," growls Dr. Murray Bowen, psychiatrist and director of the Family Center at Georgetown University in Washington, D.C., a center highly respected in the study of the family and its problems. "You want to hear a formula. There ain't any. You can't tell anyone how to do it. Let's say people—not just husbands—need an activity outside the relationship they're in. No focus on each other. Some people have more aptitude for this than others."

"What kind of people?" I want to know.

Dr. Bowen makes noises like an angry lion.

"I told you. I know no answers. I make no guesses."

I'm beginning to like this man. No trade jargon. No easy answers after thirty years of observing the difficulties people encounter in their relationships or in their life situation, the problems they drag home that change their thinking and maybe even their personalities.

"Look up 'self' in the dictionary," he says, "the differentiation of self. The immature have the most trouble. It can be total hell. In most families there's someone who can comprehend this."

"Are you married?" I asked him.

"Oh, sure."

"Is she supportive?"

He made some noise that I took to mean she was. He seemed to imply that this was good.

"I'll be at this twenty more years," he says. He's seventy-one now.

"I can understand that," I told him. "I love my work too."

He grunted.

"I don't know anything about retirement," I told him. "My father didn't exactly retire, and my husband worked until the day he fell dead."

"Died before it came time?"

"Sort of. He worked for himself. Writers don't retire."

"Too bad."

I didn't give him any trouble over that, but I don't see it that way. As he pointed out, some people have more aptitude. And special circumstances keep arising.

I looked up "self" in the dictionary. The primary definition was "a person considered with respect to complete individuality or separate identity."

There is no doubt that retirement, no matter how many protests you hear, is a landmark event in our lives, and from it spread ripples that profoundly affect people. When Kenneth Bernard, playwright and English teacher at Long Island University, wrote an article for *Newsweek* in which he referred to retirement as "descent into second class citizenship," one thousand letters vilifying him, cheering him, and generally setting him straight, descended on his doorstep. Again and again, the writers started by saying they had never written a letter to the editor on any subject before. What happens to people when they stop working is a hot subject.

Of course Bernard didn't mince words. He said flat out that "once retired you're one with blacks, Hispanics, the handicapped, homosexuals, jailbirds, the insane, the retarded, children and women. America's Third World hordes." No one could accuse him of understatement.

"I don't know why anyone would want to retire," he said

when I talked to him. "You've been working all your life, and your heart, your bowels, your mind keep time with a routine. It's like running into a brick wall full speed. No body or mind was meant to stop like that. Things have to go wrong—your heart, your bowels, your mind. It's the first giant step to the cemetery."

Not so, shouted many of the letter writers. One especially angry letter, postmarked Sun City, California, taunted Bernard for his harsh New York climate and boasted of the three golf courses, two large swimming pools, gym, "and various other activities" available near her house, which is set on "a large lot." "Eat your heart out," she advised Bernard. A letter writer in San Jose, California, remarked that all three hundred members of his branch of "Sons in Retirement" were "happy men . . . None of us is despised by our families." He and all his friends "had free passes on the county transit, passes honored for discounts in eight other transits. What better could you ask for?" he inquired.

Not much hint of happy, well-adjusted mates came through in the letters, though one letter, again from California, came from a sixty-year-old retiree who married a "twenty-nine-year-old beauty" and at sixty-one stood by in the delivery room while their son was born. He plays tennis, "makes waves. Makes love."

Do these people protest too much? Bernard thinks so, and so do I.

Bernard thinks it's interesting how often retirement was justified in these letters by the fact that the writer can now do all the things he or she wanted to do, as if life before retirement was a form of servitude. He likewise points out that, again and again, fulfillment in retirement revolved for these people around essentially meaningless activities or a pretty thorough indulgence in pleasure, idleness. "I was nefariously linked with the Protestant ethic," he says.

"Oh, my God, Kenneth Bernard," wrote a Longboat Key,

Florida, woman, "you are right—what more can anyone say!"
"There are no tribal aspects left where those who do not work
have a place," writes a woman in Fort Wayne, Indiana.

Can we see behind the words into the lives of these people and into their marriages and the thoughts of their wives?

"Women are far better equipped to withstand the perils
of this kind of change," Bernard says. "But their husbands'
self-esteem suffers. They get in the way of their wives, and
it generates anger."

Is it then the party line emanating from the retirement
communities?

"This has nothing to do with life; it is all meaningless
filler," he says.

12

What's Right
About Husbands?

Husbands, of course, have their failings, as do wives, and they don't come with a lifetime guarantee. Still, hardly anyone disputes that they are nice to have. Even those women who find their husbands less than satisfactory do not look you in the eye and demand to know who needs a husband. It's no longer a stigma to be without a husband, but marriage is better, warmer, closer, more reassuring than going it alone. The singles of the world know that marriage is better.

A whole generation of women is experimenting with the idea that a live-in lover is all that is necessary. Fear of commitment, that poor, overworked, exhausted word, is keeping a raft of young women and men from making it legal. Scars from previous encounters are slow to heal, and who needs the law's stamp anyway? Whose business is it?

Ruut Veenhoven, a Dutch sociologist from Rotterdam, wrote his Ph.D. dissertation on "Conditions of Happiness." He studied the literature on the subject in thirty-two countries, and one of his conclusions was that married people are happier than single people. Happier and live longer. Statistics from the National Center for Health Statistics report that for both men and women single people have a higher death rate than married. They also, according to Frances Kobrin and Gerry Hendershot, two sociologists from Brown University, report higher levels of happiness.

The scientific papers have examined this longevity statistic from every aspect, from added danger of suicide to catching the fatal disease of the dying mate, but what it may possibly all boil down to is loneliness. The unmarried female comes out slightly better than her male counterpart in the mortality statistics, but this is the age of fear of commitment, and it's more fashionable than it once was to go it alone. How better to find out who you are? And if you do find someone with whom you think it might work, let's try it on for size and see if it floats.

"Man, you must be kidding about love! I think our young college kids have really latched on to something. Why get married when you can simply screw your young chick and nobody gets hurt?. In the end you owe her nothing and she owes you nothing."

It's a verbatim quote from a comment made to Dr. James Lynch by a thirty-five-year-old steelworker in Baltimore. Dr. Lynch uses it in his introduction to his book on the medical consequences of loneliness, *The Broken Heart*. It speaks volumes about the social climate, disruption of old cultural patterns, and the examining of what were once considered fundamentals.

The reason for getting married, of course, is love. It's not a word much used these days, and it's debased in the current euphemism for sex, "making love." It might be that it's more apt to flourish in an atmosphere in which nobody is just testing the wind, and both, at least at the moment, think it will last forever. I think it is worth something to stand up in the company of your friends and swear that in this uncertain world, in full knowledge of the horrible divorce statistics, as near as it is possible for things to last forever, this love will endure. It takes nerve and a certain optimism in the face of known facts, and I'm inclined to tell the steelworker that it matters.

I come out squarely for husbands. Look at their record and you'll see what great partners they are. A permanent relationship fosters nice things. Like division of labor that leaves you free to feel there is no need for you to learn how to eject bats, understand the cause of the alarming noise in the hood of your elderly car, stare down headwaiters, or get out of bed at night if there is doubt the heat was turned off under the coffee. And husbands, having made the ultimate commitment, can be leaned on emotionally, a true luxury you can't find just anywhere. Knowing you and your fears better than anyone in the world, they are in a position to pooh-pooh things that haunt you, closet terrors that look embarrassing when brought out in the daylight but nevertheless have long claws and teeth. Husbands are quite sure the dog's indigestion is not the result of poisoning, that the truck driver behind you will not suffer brake failure in his sixteen-wheel rig and run you down from sheer malice, and that you do not suffer from an incurable disease. Of course they know nothing about any of these things, but that doesn't matter at all.

Then there's the whole amorphous set of wavelengths that extend beyond the boundary and realm of the voice. Without a husband, whose eye do you catch when someone says something stupid? Gerry Cullinan, who introduced me to my husband and was for years his partner, said it nicely. They were close friends, and a partnership is, of course, in a way a sort of a marriage. "I don't gotta use words when I talk to Booth," said Gerry.

I'm bullish on husbands. The balance of provider/dependent is growing obsolete, and with this change not only wives but husbands become more interesting. "Being a husband is a full time job," said Arnold Bennett, and he would probably be interested to see how husbands today have stretched and altered traditional ideas of husbands' business.

Only a little more than a hundred years ago wives in some circles addressed their husbands as "Mr."

Husbands, while taking more time to get around to being husbands, are doing a better job of it. The divorce rate of the 1970s is showing signs of abating, and beyond question husbands are taking more time for the care of their children. Right from the birth itself they are getting involved in what their fathers considered to be women's work. You may laugh when you hear about paternity leave, but it's a straw in the wind. And let's not forget the rising tide of husbands who are proud of their ability as chefs.

"Happy families are all alike," said Tolstoy. "Every unhappy family is unhappy in its own way." The divorce courts and the marriage counselors hear about the husbands who desert, the philanderers, the immature, the drunks. The husbands who are decent, generous, and loving don't make the gossip columns. But they're there. I was married to one. "It's hard to measure anyone else against your husband," said Joan.

I think it's possible that husbands, emancipated from their ancient role of sole economic provider, will have more time to develop qualities they might otherwise be too busy or too tired to think about. They will have time to consider things that escaped their notice before, time for exploring new balances and understanding, time for developing sensitivities the feminists have assured them they lack. There will be more dialogue that matters.

The answer is yes, Virginia—or Linda, was it, who wondered why any woman marries—husbands are nice to have. They are inclined to outlast lovers, and they make an apartment a home. Having taken that bold step, the choice of marriage, they are not so easily discouraged by difficulties balanced out in a long-run relationship. Husbands have already made promises lovers are not ready for.

And of course they make nice fathers for children.

In America we are careless of words. We bastardize them, overwork them until they are debased and have lost their power, misuse them, undervalue them. Often it is the foreign born, who think before they speak, who give the sort of strength and power and originality to our own language that makes us sit up straight.

I remember an evening in my favorite pan-Asian restaurant when the conversation among friends flowed easily and the talk turned to husbands. Everyone present but me was married, and I posed the stock question: Are husbands necessary in the scheme of things?

On my right sat a high-born Vietnamese woman married to an American. They had lived here for all the years of their marriage, perhaps a dozen or more. She listened gravely, her strong, beautiful face attentive.

"Husbands," she said finally. "I tell mine that that piece of meat between his legs is not the important thing. I can get that anywhere." Here an eloquent shrug.

"But when I can look into his mind" (and here she put an elegant long-fingered hand on her forehead) "and into his heart" (here on her breast) "and find love—that is important, that I value. And that I will fight to keep."

And that, of course, is what's right about husbands.

Index